To Eric
&
Cheryl,

My Life in
Dog Years

Love,

Also by Rita Rudner

MEMOIR

Rita Rudner's Guide to Men

Naked Beneath My Clothes

I Still Have It... I Just Can't Remember Where
I Put It: Confessions of a Fiftysomething

FICTION

Tickled Pink: A Comic Novel

Turning the Tables: A Novel

My Life in Dog Years

A memoir by Rita Rudner

a Villa Romana Book

First published in the United States in 2022 by Villa Romana Books,
a division of Renaissance Literary & Talent
Beverly Hills, CA

Copyright © Rita Rudner 2022

ISBN: 978-1-950369-62-1

Contents

I would like to dedicate this book to Martin Bergman, who is not only my husband, but also my lawyer, my accountant, my co-writer, my best friend and most importantly, my phone finder.

I would also like to dedicate this book to Molly Bergman, my lovely daughter who makes me proud to be her mother every day and always tells me when I'm wearing my clothes backwards and inside out.

Acknowledgments

I would like to thank the following people:

Danielle Bowen, for reading this book in its original form. That is a true friend!

Saralee Kroll, for walking her dog, Diva, with Twinkle and me for 12 years.

My literary agent, Alan Nevins, who is not only supportive and intelligent, but also very good looking.

My agent-agent, Steve Levine, for all of his excellent agenting (also intelligent and good looking).

Debby Miller and Alison Kaplan for being there for my daughter while she is attending college.

Santana Diaz for always being there for my family.

Jacklyn Saferstein-Hansen, my copy-editor, for correcting my spelling, grammar, lack of time specificity and tenses. That wasn't easy.

Elaine Thut, who designed and laid out the whole book and has to work for Alan Nevins. That also can't be easy.

David Jakle for taking such great photos of Betsy and me that I'm still not sure we chose the right one for the cover.

"The Little Red Dog" for saving Betsy's life.

Dr. Corey Brown and Dr. Robert Futeron for saving mine.

And finally, my audiences, who have been coming to see my shows now for 35 years.

A heartfelt thank you.

Introdogtion

My life can be divided up by the lives of my five dogs: my German shepherd; my Afghan/poodle/and whatever else might have been arbitrarily mixed in there; my wheaton/sheepdog/Irish wolfhound/Tibetan terrier/bathmat; my supposed Chinese crested powder-puff (I know...I'd never heard of that breed either); and my current dog, who I think is a poodle/terrier mix and who I'm calling a Perrier.

There have been periods when the extensive travel schedule that show business demands has dictated a dog-less existence, but during the majority of my life I have depended on the steady, non-judgmental, immensely-satisfying love that only dogs can bring.

My first dog, a German shepherd puppy that I named Tiny (I was evidently unaware how big she eventually would become), was essential to both my father and me during the difficult years of my mother's illness.

My second dog, Agatha, was my constant companion when I lived alone in New York in my teens. Agatha cheered me up through the onslaught of rejections that I faced both from men and trying to find work as a dancer.

Dog number three, Bonkers, was my husband's and my surrogate first child. He was also in my comedy act and played Las Vegas with me for years.

Dog number four, Twinkle, was my perpetual baby for 13 years. She was my first small dog and loved to be picked up and cuddled.

My current dog, Betsy, is still very much a puppy and possesses many of Twinkle's characteristics. Abandoned on the streets of Los Angeles during the pandemic, she was found with a broken leg and an unproduced screenplay. She is under my desk as I type this, anxious for me to finish so we can play.

I don't think this book is going to be exactly what you expect. Hopefully, you will find some of it amusing, but life is not always funny. I've had difficult times, just like everybody else. I believe the way you deal with those challenges and the decisions you make during those periods dictate your life's trajectory.

Also, it helps if you have a dog.

The Chapter Before Chapter One

I don't care where you're from, Las Vegas is the opposite of it.

"Five minutes."

"Okay. Thanks, Chris."

My stage manager leaves, busy with a message being relayed into his headphones.

I'm sitting backstage in the Las Vegas star dressing room that's been built specifically for me. It's pink and feminine and silly. Memorabilia and photos from my career as a comedian and a dancer decorate its walls. I've been performing in this newly-constructed theater for twelve months now.

I get up from the shockingly pink sofa and check out my new, over-priced gown, bought especially for tonight's one-year anniversary show, in the full-length, art-deco mirror. My dog Bonkers comes over to give my hand a good-luck lick.

The door to my dressing room opens again.

"It's nuts out there," my husband Martin reports. "The casino's given out pink feather boas and free MargaRitaRudners. Your dad is drunk and itchy."

How did I get here and how lucky am I? My own theater in Las Vegas; a multi-million-dollar, multi-year contract; celebrating my 14th wedding anniversary with my English husband as we prepare our 30th floor penthouse overlooking the Las Vegas Strip for the arrival of the baby we're about to adopt.

"Have a good show, darling," says Martin supportively. "I'll see you afterwards."

It's April 2002. I've performed 355 sold-out solo comedy shows in this theater so far. Time for show #356.

What would my mother think if she could see me now?

THE TINY
YEARS

I always thought I was adopted when I was growing up because I don't look like anyone in my family. I look a little like my grandmother now, because I have brown hair and blue eyes and she has blue hair and brown eyes.

That's my mother's mother. She's a very tough cookie. Really. She's buried three husbands. Two of them were just napping.

One

My problem with memoirs is the early chapters invariably contain too much back-story. I want to read about the person the book is about, not many pages about the intricate details of the lives of his or her great, great, great grandparents. Luckily, I don't know much about my family history, and I have no desire to commission an online search that will tell me more; I don't understand what difference it will make to my life if I know my great uncle on my mother's side was a librarian in Poland.

Here's what I know about what happened before I was born: my dad was the youngest of three children and was born in Hurleyville, New York, which is a small town in the Catskill Mountains. His father owned Rudner's department store and that's where my parents met. My dad worked there and my mom, who was born in Brooklyn but came up to the mountains every summer, kept visiting the store to buy thread.

Eventually my dad left to fight in World War Two, although, I wouldn't exactly call it fighting. On the bus to New Jersey, an officer asked if anyone could type. My father raised his hand and that night learned how to type. He suffered zero typing injuries and after the war my parents married and moved down to Miami because my father never wanted to be cold again. He'd decided against California; his older brother lived there and my father didn't like the woman his brother had married.

My father went to law school courtesy of the G.I. Bill while my mother found a job in a banana factory. Baby bananas arrived on ships from South America and were placed in radiated rooms until they grew up to be adult bananas. My mother's job was to check regularly on the immature bananas and, when she felt they were ready to go out into the world, put them in boxes so they could be delivered to various supermarkets. There you have the life of a banana in the 1940s. A little more interesting than finding out your great uncle was a librarian in Poland, but maybe not.

My father became a divorce lawyer. After he had successfully represented numerous clients in toxic marital relationships, and after my mother had raised many thousands of bananas, they found they had saved enough money to build a small house next door to a railroad track. That's where I was born. I lived there until I was four, and the only memory I've retained about the house is my mom being on the phone when the sound of a passing train roared through our living room. She would shout, "Hang on a second" while burying the receiver in the sofa cushions until the arrival of the caboose. That's a word not used enough these days. I'm going to write it again just because I like it. Caboose.

As a girl, my mother wanted to be a dancer. Her father deemed it unacceptable for a female to be a dancer on the stage and so that was the end of that dream. That frustration no doubt had much to do with my mom taking me to my first ballet class when I was four. I fell in love. All I wanted to do with my life from that moment on was to be a dancer. It was an all-consuming passion, marred only by my mother taking me to the doctor to be vaccinated. I had the choice of the shot being administered on my arm or on my leg. My mother chose my leg. It became infected and had to be re-done, leaving a visible scar on my thigh.

"How can I be a dancer with this scar on my leg?" I cried. Oh, what a big deal it was. I still have the scar. Turned out it wasn't a big deal.

Just when we were becoming used to the train speeding through our living room, there was a knock at our door. My father opened it and found a man with a clipboard. They talked for a while, the man left and my dad walked back into the living room holding a letter. The government wanted to buy our house. The railroad was being replaced by a highway and our house was directly in the way. This cheap piece of land was suddenly valuable; we were in the wrong place at the right time.

My father scoured better neighborhoods for a place to build a new house. For some reason, he didn't look for a *For Sale* sign or call a realtor. Instead, he drove up and down looking for a place he would want to live. While most people in Miami covet a property with an ocean view my father, honorary president of the *Worst-Case Scenario Club*, looked for high land.

"The hurricanes are gonna knock all these houses out," he pronounced. "If I wanna see the ocean, I'll go look at the ocean. Then I'll go home."

He took us to see an empty piece of land connected to an old house on a quiet street in an area of Miami called Coconut Grove. It was overgrown with weeds and there was a derelict bird bath in the middle of the lot.

"This is where I'm building our new house," he announced triumphantly.

He had knocked on the door of the old property to which the land was connected. He figured that since it was an old house, there was a good chance it might have an old owner. Given it was run down, the owner might need money. Plus, because it had land connected to it that was solely providing bathing facilities to birds, the owner might want to sell said land. Turned out, he was correct on all counts. He offered the elderly woman who owned the house an all-cash deal and she sold him her lot. As a lawyer, he was able to handle the necessary paperwork associated with the purchase himself. He enjoyed the process so much that he ended his divorce lawyer career and became a real estate lawyer, finding representing property to be much less depressing than representing acrimonious husbands and wives. Land didn't argue and houses didn't hate each other.

My father designed the house with very little input from my mother or anyone else. It was a two-bedroom, two-bathroom house with a one-car garage. My father wouldn't let my mother learn how to drive. He was convinced that women's brains were not wired for serious activities. I still remember him telling me, "Women are decorative. They don't have the concentration that driving takes." Don't hate him. He did evolve later in life, particularly when I started to support him.

My father's personality was devoid of rationality. He would read about a tuna fish diet and come home with fifty cans of tuna fish. Of course, he then proceeded to eat one can of tuna fish and decided it wasn't for him. He saw an exercise machine on television and ordered four of them. He tried it once and then proclaimed it, "Garbage."

"Why don't you try something before you go all in? Most normal people try things first," I asked.

"I ain't interested in being normal," he replied.

We moved into the house just before I turned five. That was also when I entered the first grade. I was too young, but my dad decided my mother would be his secretary in his new real estate business and there was nobody home to take care of me. So off I went.

It was around this age that I noticed I didn't have a dog. My friends had dogs. I loved dogs. I wanted a dog. My mother wanted a dog. She had a Boston terrier growing up whom she adored. My father was dead set against it. Dogs were dirty, sloppy, needy wastes of time. I had acquiesced on many issues, but not on this one. It was to be a long climb.

My first dog was a fish. She was bright orange and I named her Cookie. I liked Cookie. I fed her every morning and watched her eat her food with her fish mouth, but it was very apparent to me that Cookie wasn't a dog. My second dog was a turtle, followed by a parakeet and a chicken. Yes, a chicken. I went horseback riding on a farm and they were giving away adorable baby chicks. I named my chicken Wally. Wally was cute for a while, until he got out of his cage. He quickly went back to his farm, and I had to accept the fact that you can't housebreak a chicken. (I'll bet you've never read that sentence before).

One day my mother spotted an advertisement in the local paper. A woman was selling toy poodle puppies. My parents left me with a neighbor, and a few hours later they arrived back home with a tiny, copper-colored poodle puppy that I named Puffy. Things went wrong almost immediately. Puffy wouldn't eat, she didn't have any energy and her bodily functions were, let's just say, erratic. Puffy died in a matter of days. My father notified the Board of Health and after an investigation they discovered that the woman's puppy business was in violation of a plethora of health codes and shut her down. The three of us were so affected by this little puppy's death that my father proclaimed, "No More Dogs!!!"

By now, in addition to ballet, my mother had added piano lessons to the Rita schedule. With ballet, I had natural ability. With piano, the opposite was true. Luckily, I stuck with it because, as it happened, my piano teacher bred German shepherds. Mr. Maddern brought a German shepherd puppy over to our house and we all agreed she would be the new member of our family. I guess subconsciously I was still hoping for a small dog because, as I said earlier, I named her Tiny.

"The dog lives outside," my father announced. And she did. For about an hour. We saw her little face peering through the screen door and my mother and I said nothing until my father re-announced, "She stays on the porch. She doesn't enter the rest of the house."

Gradually, she was allowed in the kitchen, den, bedrooms and anywhere else she decided to go. The place she went the least? Outside.

The dog's arrival generated something that took both my mom and me by surprise. Tiny released feelings in my father that we never knew were lurking inside of him; a tenderness that neither one of us had ever seen. Before he went to sleep, my father would sit down on the bed and call Tiny over and discuss his day with her. He also asked her about her day: whether she had enjoyed her dinner, had a nice nap or had seen any birds. Often, he made up poems at night for her amusement. From the day Tiny entered our lives my dad was a gentler, more understanding human being. Tiny protected me and loved my mom, but she was dedicated to my dad.

Tiny was a natural guard dog, much to my friends' consternation, especially when they slept over. Once my friend, Cyndi took a hair brush out of my hand and Tiny cornered her. She didn't growl and she never bit anyone. She just stared people down.

"What should I do?" frozen, frightened Cyndi wailed, as Tiny glared at her intensely.

"Just give me the brush back and it will be fine."

Cyndi handed me the brush and Tiny walked back to her corner, pretending to have stopped paying attention. However, I could tell she still had her dog antennae erect just in case Cyndi pulled another fast one. After that, I spent sleepover nights at Cyndi's house where Cyndi had a Schnauzer. Schnitzel was much more relaxed than Tiny, although she did chew my retainer.

My ballet friend, Charlene, also had a Tiny sleepover-scare when we decided to raid the kitchen at 2:00 in the morning. As we entered, Tiny ran out of my parent's bedroom and wanted to know the story. She let me pass, but stood sentry in front of Charlene until I assured her that Charlene was not an enemy agent. No alarm system was needed with Sergeant Tiny guarding the house.

I met Charlene when I was eight years old and we became as close as sisters. I met Cyndi when I was ten and we are in constant touch. I haven't met Julie yet, but will in about ten years. Although I don't see them as often as I would like because we all live in different states now, they are still only a phone call away. They don't have to read this book. They know everything.

My mother's domestic talents didn't extend to the kitchen. Spaghetti with butter and ketchup and Campbell's vegetable soup mixed with rice were two of her favorites. She once tried to heat up a can of corn in the oven and it exploded. For some time, we found pieces of corn in strange places throughout the kitchen.

Since my mom didn't know how to drive, I spent a lot of time with her on buses. She would leave my father's office and take a bus to meet me after school and then we took two more buses to my ballet class. My mother would sit with Charlene's mother and watch the ballet class. The ballet teacher, Mr. Millenoff, was a tough-talking Russian who loved poking our legs with his stick when they weren't straight enough to please him. Mr. Millenoff also had an ancient, lumpy German shepherd who slowly shuffled behind him on flat paws wherever he went, so I was never really scared of my teacher; I knew he had a softer side.

My mother made a lot of my clothes. She had a dear friend, Selma, and the two of them bought the same patterns together to save money. As a consequence, Selma's daughter Harriet and I often wore identical dresses. Selma, Harriet and I re-connected a few years ago – as I write this, Selma recently celebrated her 98th birthday. When we next meet up, for old time's sake, maybe Harriet and I should wear matching dresses!

My mother was a very likeable, socially-adept person. She possessed that quality that makes everyone feel special. You always knew you could confide in my mom about anything and she would understand and try her best to be helpful. My dad was the antithesis; innately suspicious, always thinking people had an angle and always on his guard in case he had to pounce (kind of like Tiny, which is probably why they got along so well.)

My parents were very good friends with a doctor and his wife who had two sons I played with often. I'm changing everybody's names because I don't want anyone to be upset. I'll try to keep the characters straight. Let's call the doctor "Stan" and his wife "Babette." No, I don't like those names. Let's call the doctor "Milton" and his wife "Grace." I like that better. Let's call their two sons "Sally" and "Mona." Only kidding. "David" and "Carl." I feel their last name coming to me and it's...... "Schienman." Too many letters to type. "Stein." Better.

My mother and Babette, I mean Grace, were very good friends. I remember them laughing constantly. I especially remember the time we were leaving a winding parking lot exit from the top floor. Grace had just learned to drive and could not maneuver the car very well. She had never driven in a circle and managed to creep down the circular exit bumping into walls at every turn. It got so bad, the three of us collapsed on the seats in fits of hysterics. The cars backed up behind us didn't find it so funny. Neither did Stan, I mean Milton.

Our families dined together often. People liked my mom so much they even put up with her cooking. One evening after dinner, my mother disappeared into the bedroom with Milton.

"It's nothing," he said, as they returned to the living room. "We'll keep an eye on it."

This disappearing into the bedroom after dinner went on every couple of weeks for the next six months or so. One night, after the Steins left the house, I heard my father screaming at my mother.

"This is ridiculous. You have to go to a different doctor."

She did. It was too late.

As luck wouldn't have it, Milton, a person who adored my mother and was doing his best to take care or her, inadvertently contributed to her demise. In his defense, not that much was known about breast cancer in the 1950s. "We'll keep an eye on it" is even a phrase that I've heard doctors say today. In this case, that phrase proved fatal.

My mother was put into the hospital and underwent a radical mastectomy. I was six. Neither my father or my mother told me what was happening. I was left to observe and draw my own conclusions. My mother was in and out of hospitals for the next eight years.

My father did not believe in any kind of insurance. "I ain't sending any money to those crooks," I recall him pronouncing. We didn't have burglary, fire, flood or health insurance. Consequently, as medical bills poured in, money became very tight. We coped as best we could. My father worked longer and longer hours and I would take buses home from school; good thing I was familiar with buses. When my mom was home, I helped her do whatever it was that she needed to accomplish and when she was in the hospital, I made myself dinner, did my homework and waited until my dad arrived home to take me to ballet class. They say that every comedian has gone through some sort of trauma. I guess I conform to the stereotype.

Although we were a Jewish family, we were not a religious household. We never went to temple. We did celebrate the major holidays, usually at a friend or relative's house. Once my mother became sick, though, any nod towards Judaism quickly disappeared.

A problem arose in the summer when school was out. What to do with Rita? When I was nine, I was forced to leave my sick mother to go to a summer camp in North Carolina for two months. For most kids it would have been a privilege, but for me at that time it was quite traumatic. I had never been away from home and two months felt inordinately long. I wrote letters pleading to come home. Gradually, I made friends and adjusted to my rural surroundings. Even though I missed ballet, I loved horseback riding and the Blue Ridge Mountains were a magical, stunning backdrop.

The kids that were at camp for two months were allowed one day in between months when their parents could come and visit them. Everybody's parents in my cabin were coming, except for mine. I wrote another letter, pleading to come home; one month was enough, I argued. My dad replied that it was impossible and he would see me at the airport when the second month was over.

As my friends' parents arrived, I remember sitting on my bunk bed, playing a guitar and trying to look busy. Then my counselor, Patty, said, "Rita, I think there's someone here to see you."

It was my mom. She had struggled to get on a plane and get herself to camp on visiting day. I'll never forget seeing her smiling face and watching her walk slowly up the dirt road to the cabin. I got to spend the whole day with my mother. She saw me horseback ride and swim. She came to mess hall for lunch and met my friends. It was a great day.

As my mother's health deteriorated, the only constant positive in my life was ballet. My bff Charlene and I switched to a different ballet school and we were both accepted into a Cuban ballet company called *Ballet Concerto*. I was 11 and Charlene was 13. Almost every evening and every weekend we were at the ballet school learning the great ballets. Sonia and Marta, the directors of the school, hired professional dancers to dance the leads and twice a year we performed a ballet at Dade County Auditorium. We danced *Swan Lake*, *The Nutcracker*, *La Sylphide*, *Coppélia* and a few others that I can't remember. Sadly, my mother never got to see any of them.

Ballet is a profession that not only demands total dedication and a stultifying work ethic, but also that you be born with the correct physique. Charlene was. I wasn't. My feet never had the correct arches. It wasn't for lack of trying. I rolled my feet on coke bottles; slept with weights over my toes; bent my feet furiously for hours at a time, hoping they would decide to curve correctly. I also needed to be thinner. I tried bulimia, but it didn't work for me. Thankfully, I found it too icky. I starved myself, but developed migraine headaches. I cut out carbs and my energy level plummeted. I wasn't overweight, but I was too curvy for ballet. The male dancers did not look forward to lifting me, and I never really trusted that they were going to catch me. As much as I loved ballet, I began to realize it was more likely musicals would feature heavily in my future. I began taking tap and jazz classes plus singing lessons. Oh yes, and acrobatics. I was determined to get on Broadway, even if I had to do handstands.

When I moved to New York to be a dancer, I lived right off Central Park. I couldn't actually see the park, but if I concentrated, I could hear the screams for help.

Two

A hospital bed arrived and was placed in my parents' bedroom. My mother could no longer be operated on. Up until age six, I remember being a pretty selfish, spoiled kid. That's not unusual - a parent's world usually revolves around the children. However, for me, after six, my world revolved around my mother. As I mentioned, my father was not what you would call an introspective human being. Forget counseling or therapy. Every time I asked a question, like, "Why is this happening?" or "Is mommy ever going to get better?" he snapped, "I'm doing my best. What else do you want me to do?"

I was still allowed to have friends over to our house, but the door to my mother's bedroom now always remained closed. None of my friends were allowed to see her. If I wanted to ask her a question, I slipped into her room and closed the door quickly behind me. Tiny was always there by her bed. The dog came out for walks and food, but otherwise she guarded my mom.

By this time, my dad had sold the family silverware to keep up with health payments. We couldn't afford a nurse, so a friend's daughter who was out of work stayed with my mom during the day until I arrived home from school. I'm sorry this sounds so grim, but that's the way it was.

My mom had one rule that I had to adhere to. Whenever I left the house, I was never allowed to say, "Goodbye." I always had to say, "See you later." We never talked about her dying, but one night, while I was lying next to her, I heard her say, "I wish you didn't love me so much." That, of course, wasn't a possibility.

She died a few days later. Tiny and I were by her bed and we just waited for my dad to come home from the office. I was 13.

The rest of that year is a bit of a blur. I remember the funeral. My mom was dressed in her favorite green dress. I wore a green dress as well. Looking over to my father I saw one singular tear running down his cheek. That was the extent of his outer grief. Who knows what was going on inside? At the cemetery we walked quite a distance to my mom's burial spot. It was located at the far outer corner. I asked my father why he'd picked that spot. He said, "I only wanted people on one side of her." That didn't make much sense. My mother was a people-person. I think it was because his plot was right next to hers and, even in death, my father didn't want to be bothered by other dead people. I guess he thought they might have a party and disturb him.

We never spoke to the Steins again. My father cut off all of my mother's friends and their children and I never saw them again either. Luckily, he didn't cut off my friends. They were always there for me. Here I shall do my version of an Oscar acceptance speech: "I don't need to thank everyone who supported me. They know who they are."

I poured my energy into my obsessive desire to go to New York and become a dancer on Broadway. I thought of nothing else. The early edition of the Miami Herald sometimes had auditions in the entertainment section for shows on Miami Beach. I found one for *Stop the World - I Want to Get Off* at the Deauville Hotel. I told my father I would be going to the audition, even though it was scheduled on a school day. Remarkably, he agreed to let me skip school. I took three buses to Miami Beach and got a job as a dancer in the show. I was still only 13. The producers only had to pay me $100 a week because I was non-union. Looking back, that might have had something to do with my employment. My father lied to the school and said I was sick. He had my work sent home and that was how I graduated the 10th grade.

1967 was spent trying to figure out how to get to New York City. As much as I loved Tiny, I needed to escape the oppressive memories contained in that house. By the middle of the school year, I had developed a plan. Charlene and her mother traveled to New York City the summer before in order for Charlene to take lessons from world-class, New York ballet teachers. They were going again the next summer. I asked if I could join them.

"Wait until we get settled and see if the place we have rented is big enough," Charlene's mother advised. I slept with my hand on the white princess phone receiver next to my bed. It wasn't a comfortable position, but entirely necessary so I could answer on the first ring. On the third night of their trip to New York, the phone rang.

"The place is big enough. When can you come?" Charlene squealed.

I was on a plane a week later. That was the beginning of my love affair with New York City. The three of us lived in an "unusual" hotel on 86th Street and Broadway. Every evening there were various women loitering on the steps of the hotel. all wearing wigs and tight dresses. Every day Charlene and I went to dance classes from 10:00 in the morning until 6:00 in the evening. At night we attended ballet performances and shows. We learned how to take subways and buses to our lessons. (As I write this, I'm realizing just how much of my early career depended on public transportation.)

We bought the show business papers and went to a few auditions. Our destinies immediately became evident. Charlene got a call-back to the Radio City Ballet Company and I got a call-back to a Broadway show. We didn't attend the call-backs because we were too young to work, but it was encouraging all the same.

One night, while having dinner in our apartment, a telegram arrived for me. My heart started beating faster and I was afraid to open it. Had something happened to my father? Was I now an orphan? I opened the telegram. Something had indeed happened to my father.

"Hi Dolly," the telegram read ("Dolly" was my father's pet name for me). "Just wanted to let you know. Got married today. Very nice woman. Dad."

At the end of the summer, Charlene, her mother and I boarded a Miami-bound plane. No crazy people had blown up planes yet and loved ones were still allowed to meet you at the gate. As I de-planed (love that word), I saw my father. He was wearing pastel pants and a white belt topped off with a flowered shirt. He had never dressed like that in his life. Standing next to him was a very tall, dark-haired lady whom I suspected of picking out his outfit.

"Hi Dolly. This is Dagny. Dagny, this is Rita Carol."

"Dagny," I thought. "What kind of name is "Dagny"?"

Dagny, it turned out, was Norwegian for "Dagny." Dagny was 50 years old and had never been married before. She worked at a court reporting service that was doing some book-keeping for my father. He had known her for about a month. Conversation in the car ride from the airport was understandably stilted.

Tiny was there to greet me when we arrived home. She didn't leave my side. She followed me around and looked up at me with eyes that said, "Thank goodness you are home. Something is wacky in this house." Maybe I read too much into her expression, but I'm sure I saw my dog frown.

Things swiftly went from chilly to frostbite. As I walked down the hall to my room, I couldn't help noticing the wallpaper change. Huge pink flamingos now lined the walls, alternating with electric green palm fronds.

"What happened here?" I said, undiplomatically.

"It's our new wall covering. Isn't it beautiful?" said Dagny in a baby voice. Dagny was over six feet tall, and I think she thought her baby voice made her appear smaller.

"Oh yes," I lied in a high, lying voice.

I wandered into my room and noticed there were a few things missing. There were no lights. All of my lamps were missing.

"We needed more light in other parts of the house," Dagny explained.

"Okay, but I'm home now. Can I have some lights in my room?"

My father quickly jumped in. "We'll fix it tomorrow."

I found a lamp in the den and placed it in my room. I began unpacking in the gloom. It was then I noticed my bed was not made. If I had married someone who had a teenage daughter whose mother had died and I was trying to make a good impression, I would have made the bed. But maybe that's just me.

Tiny and I decided to check out the living room to see if there were any more flamingos. We didn't spot any birds, but in the far corner of the room sat some modern furniture that was unfamiliar; an orange couch, a chrome lamp, a glass coffee table. In the near corner was my mother's furniture; an off-white, antique sofa, a wooden coffee table, upholstered chairs. Each wife had her own corner. Things were becoming stranger and stranger.

I was in the kitchen when I saw Dagny dragging bedding onto the porch. My father joined me at the kitchen table.

"Where is Dagny going?" I asked.

"She's sleeping on the porch tonight. She's not sure she wants to stay here. She says we're ganging up on her."

"Because I wanted a lamp?"

"I don't know. Just try to be nice. If she wants to go, she can go."

Tiny followed me into my bedroom and we went to confused sleep.

Dagny didn't go and we tried to get along, but it was clearly not going to work. I can report that she was kind to Tiny and my father seemed to be happy. However, it wasn't hard to figure out that I wasn't wanted on her journey, especially when I discovered her desire to adopt a baby. I decided to do 11th and 12th grades together and to get back to New York City as quickly as possible. Attempting to complete these two grades at such a young age may sound impressive, but I didn't attend a great school. The bus driver eventually became the principal (really) and you will be unsurprised to learn this fine establishment no longer exists.

The combination of frantic academic studying and the ballet company meant I was too busy to ruminate about my isolated, ruptured life. I did have some good friends. In fact, they threw me a surprise party for my 14th birthday at one of their houses. That meant a lot to me. The house had an indoor swimming pool and I thought I was just being invited for a swim date on my birthday. When I arrived, all of my friends were there to sing to me. One of their moms had thoughtfully baked me a cake. The phrase "mean girls" has become popular when referencing certain high school females. I never had that experience growing up. My friends were supportive and caring. Maybe I was just lucky.

I finished my last few school credits in summer school and graduated high school in July when I was 15. Seems crazy now, but in my upturned life, it seemed perfectly logical. Charlene had been awarded a scholarship to the Harkness Ballet, a company that had been established a couple of years earlier by Rebekah Harkness, an eccentric philanthropist and ballet enthusiast. Charlene had already graduated and moved to New York. She was living at a boarding house for girls called, St. Mary's. I applied to St. Mary's, but they were full. I'm not saying that they didn't accept me because I was Jewish, but I don't think it helped.

I had an older cousin, Arlene, who was a school teacher in New York and she found a place for me to live called the Barbizon Hotel for Women. It wasn't overly expensive and it was in a great location on the East Side of Manhattan. My father booked me in. He told me if I changed my mind and wanted to come home, then that would be fine with him. He and Dagny were arguing about adopting a baby. Dagny wasn't sure she was going to stay. Are you sensing a pattern?

Arlene met me at the airport. She was one of the few women in the Rudner family circle allowed to drive. Now all she needed was a car. We took a taxi to the Barbizon. The hotel was not what I expected. Past residents had included, among others, Lauren Bacall. Candice Bergen, Joan Crawford, Grace Kelly, Ali McGraw, Sylvia Plath, Elaine Stritch and Nancy Reagan. None of them were in the lobby. Instead, there were old ladies watching television with the volume lowered to "why bother?" It reminded me of a musty, old library with no books. Built in 1927, its architecture was a weird mix of Italian Renaissance and Gothic Revival with Islamic decorative elements. There was a huge sign on the desk: NO MEN ALLOWED. Evidently, no one was allowed to help me with my suitcases either. I dragged them into the tiny elevator and down the hall to my room. It should perhaps have been called "no room." It was a walk-in closet with a single bed in the corner and a clothing rack and a cracked sink on the side. The bathrooms and showers were down the hall.

I was a little apprehensive, but the thought of moving back home was even less appetizing. The next day I walked to St. Mary's to see Charlene. Her living quarters were much more appealing; cleaner and full of young girls trying to make it in various facets of show business. She was in the 1937 movie *Stage Door* with Ginger Rogers and Katharine Hepburn. I was in the movie *Cocoon*, with Jessica Tandy and Maureen Stapleton, 20 years before it was actually made. Charlene's routine was mapped out: the scholarship provided her with a daily schedule of classes and what she needed to accomplish. She was on her way to becoming a ballerina. I, on the other hand, was on my own and living in a haunted hotel.

My father's financial situation had bounced back and he agreed to pay for my rent as well as my classes. Thanks to my previous summer with Charlene and her mother, I knew where I was going and how to get there. The next day I was back on public transportation and on my way to ballet class.

People cope with extreme grief in different ways. Thinking back, I feel I coped with mine by exhausting myself. I took dance classes from 10:00 a.m. until dark. I remember being so tired and achy at the end of the day that I would lay in the bathtub down the hall in a complete stupor.

As far as food went, I kept protein bars in my room for breakfast and when I wasn't heating up canned Chinese food in my electric pot, I ate dinner in the coffee shop downstairs. There was one other young girl staying at the Barbizon. She was 16 and had a scholarship to the New York City Ballet School. I can't remember her name, but I remember she was skinny and had very arched feet. We ate dinner together most nights and we celebrated my 16th birthday at the coffee shop. No cake for dessert. Melon. She was on a diet.

Show Business and *Backstage* were the two papers to buy to find out about auditions. They came out on Thursday afternoon. I brought them back to my cell and studied them to see if there were any possible jobs I might be suited for. Not being in Equity meant I had to attend "Open" auditions. The union law required that producers hold open auditions even if they didn't need performers. Hundreds of girls showed up for these auditions, including me. After five months of open-call auditioning, I landed my first job.

THE AGATHA YEARS

If I were to get my own dog, I would get a seeing eye dog or a hunting dog. I don't have enough time to spend at home with my dog and I'd feel guilty. I'd just feel better if I had a dog that was involved in a career.

Three

A national tour of *Zorba,* starring John Raitt and Chita Rivera, was my first professional job in early 1970. As I stood in the line-up of the girls who were being picked for the tour, the assistant choreographer pointed at me and said, "You'll be the swing girl."

I said, "Okay." I thought it meant that I would swing in on a rope. It sounded like fun. At the first day of rehearsals, I found out it meant that I had to memorize all the parts of everyone in the chorus – both dancing and singing - and if they fell sick, I would fill in for them; talk about a learning curve.

I phoned my father and told him that I was going to go on the road with a show for a year. He seemed pleased. I guess he was just happy I still wasn't driving. He also mentioned, as he often did, that I should bring a sweater.

Zorba had recently closed on Broadway. It was a musical version by Kander & Ebb of the 1950s novel and successful film based on the friendship between Zorba and a young American man on Crete as they romantically pursue two women. This touring version was more fun and less austere than the version that had opened two years earlier, and it was hoped that it could eventually come back into New York (it didn't).

We rehearsed *Zorba* in an empty theater on Broadway. The thrill of entering a Broadway theater and knowing that I belonged and wasn't trespassing was indescribable. Hal Prince, Broadway royalty, was the director. When I wasn't learning a routine, I was able to sit in the theater and watch him direct. During rehearsals, Hal Prince was having vocal problems. He sat in a seat in the middle of the dark theatre and spoke to the on-stage actors through a megaphone, which I found wildly amusing. I'm not sure what the cast thought of me, but they were very understanding and patient with the 16-year-old kid in their midst.

The first stop on the tour was Philadelphia. Opening night, I was quite surprised when my father showed up. He was actually worried about me.

"Just wanted to make sure you were okay," he explained. He stayed the night and went back to Florida the next morning.

John Raitt had been a big star in multiple shows on Broadway. By the time this national tour went on the road, John was in his fifties and still extremely handsome. Looking back, I remember thinking that he was really old. Now I think, "He was only in his fifties! He was a baby!"

John was engaged to a beautiful woman in her twenties named Kathy who was an ex-beauty queen and a dancer. She came on tour as his dresser and mesmerized all of the stage hands by constantly showing up backstage wearing just a leotard and tights. I bet you think I'm going to write something snarky at this point. A beauty queen in her twenties in a leotard and tights and engaged to an older man? Well, Kathy was my idol. She was sweet, friendly and smart. She had luxurious long auburn hair enhanced by a fall she attached mid-head that made her hair look even more sensational. I went out and bought a fall and tried to look like her. Sadly, nobody ever mistook me for the gorgeous Kathy.

I didn't have much interaction with the stars of the show. Chita Rivera was extraordinarily talented and a little scary. The first time I went on stage for another dancer, I tried to jump too high and fell on my backside directly in front of her. Chita wasn't happy about that and mentioned it to me at the end of the show. She said I should avoid dancing in front of her ever again. She certainly had a point and I never did.

Touring the country with a show is an experience I can recommend. We spent a few weeks in each city and were able to sight-see and get a feel for our surroundings before packing up and moving on. Upon arrival in each city a sheet was posted on the bulletin board and we signed up for the hotel in the next port of call. I had a roommate, Jeanette. At 21, she was the second youngest company member. I was so happy that someone wanted to room with me. I wasn't the best conversationalist in the world, which was probably a blessing because if I had talked, I would not have known what I was talking about. One of the people on the tour had a dog. I ended up spending a lot of time with Sam, a very handsome cockapoo.

Because logic wasn't and isn't my strong point, while in San Francisco I acquired a dog. Bob, who was Sam's owner, probably wanted his dog back, so he found me one of my own. I'm not sure how it happened. Bob knew someone who knew someone who knew someone. However, happen it did, and I remember going into what was alleged to be a pet store and saw what was alleged to be an Afghan/poodle mix and immediately knew we were meant to be together. She was about six months old, and full of love, matts and worms. Fifteen dollars later, she was mine. I named her Agatha.

I don't think anyone had spent a lot of time on Agatha before I arrived in her life. She had ear infections, skin issues and a sensitive stomach. Agatha required a special dog food that I had to travel with in my suitcase. It's a good thing the airlines weren't weighing luggage back then; those cans weren't light. Agatha also needed to be house-broken. I walked her outside for hours before she peed and the moment always happened in the middle of the street. I'd kneel down in traffic to tell her what a good girl she was, while cars honked at me to get over to the sidewalk.

The singer/songwriter Bonnie Raitt is John Raitt's daughter. A few of the stage hands had rented a house in Mill Valley, a scenic city across the bay from San Francisco. Bonnie had just signed her first big record deal and a celebratory barbecue was happening at that house, with the entire cast and crew invited. I, of course, came with Agatha. The house was up a mountain and nestled in the woods.

Bonnie brought her guitar and sang the cast some of the songs that were going to be introduced on her album. We all agreed she was about to become extremely successful. We were right.

While we were all in the backyard, waiting for burgers, I was sitting with Agatha on her leash.

Bob said, "Why don't you let her off the leash? She'll stay with Sam."

I had a feeling that this wasn't in any book about dogs that I had ever read. "A puppy will stay by the side of a dog she has just met" was not a sentence that sounded familiar. But, I didn't want to appear crazy, so I let Agatha off the leash…in the backyard that butted up against the woods. I kept my eye on Agatha until I didn't. Ten minutes later, Sam was by Bob's side and Agatha was gone.

"She'll be back. She'll smell the burgers," Bob promised.

Agatha never came back. It was getting dark and Agatha was nowhere to be seen. I was crying and Bob felt super-guilty, so he jumped in his car and drove up and down the winding mountain road, looking for Agatha. I was sure that I would never see her again and couldn't believe I had been so gullible and irresponsible.

About an hour later, Bob showed up and exited the car holding an ultra-muddy Agatha. I had never been so happy to see a dirty dog in my life. I attached the leash to her collar and never let her free in an unfenced area again. How stupid was I to let a six-month-old puppy off of the leash in a strange place and how lucky was I that Bob found her?

Traveling with a dog is never easy, but finding hotels that accept dogs is next to impossible. I should have thought through the "being on the road with a dog" thing better, but if I had, I would have never known Agatha. By the end of the tour, Agatha had grown rather large. I lied on hotel sign-up sheets and said she was a poodle. That conjured up the image of a small, neat pet. The lie was half-true. She *was* half poodle. Half standard-poodle. Agatha was having to travel in an extra-large crate as she now weighed over 50 pounds.

Thankfully, we were nearing the end of the tour, and Jeanette and I and Agatha planned to be roommates in New York City.

We rented an apartment in a brownstone located in a sketchy part of the upper west side. It was a one bedroom, one window apartment and tomb-like. We bought twin beds and the rest of our furniture came from things people threw out on the street that we covered up with material. The good news was the apartment was near Central Park and Agatha needed a lot of exercise. She was a growing girl.

I began buying the show business papers and auditioning again. I was now in the Equity union, so only 50 girls showed up for a job instead of 500. After a few tries, I landed a job in the chorus of *How to Succeed in Business*. The show starred the two original Broadway actors, Bobby Morse and Rudy Vallee, and it was to be staged in, wait for it, Coconut Grove. The Coconut Grove Theatre was ten minutes from where I grew up. I saw many musicals there throughout my childhood and had always fantasized about one day being on that stage.

We rehearsed in New York and three weeks later I was getting Agatha's extra-large crate out of the brownstone basement and hailing a cab to the airport. My dad picked me up from the airport with my pal Dagny by his side. After my luggage came around, I waited for Agatha to be brought from the plane. When she finally showed up in her crate, she was fine but anxious to be out of her plastic prison. My dad laughed when he saw the hairy ball of love bouncing around the baggage claim area. Dagny said tersely, "What is that?"

When we arrived back at the house, it was a tense meeting between the two dogs. Tiny wasn't sure what was happening. There had never been another dog in the house. Agatha kept assuming the "I want to play" position. Tiny just turned and walked away.

Similarly, Dagny and I tried to become friends, but it was never going to happen. She did at some point mention that I needed to lose weight and wanted to know why I had such bad skin. That didn't help. Dagny and I had one conversation that stayed with me. She said, "Jackie Kennedy is my idol because she is flat-chested and JFK loves her anyway." She also told me that she had a vision of herself wearing a necklace that had little diamonds all around her neck. Evidently, my father had forgotten to tell her that he wasn't wealthy.

The show with Bobby and Rudy went well. The Miami Herald did a feature on me using a "local gal makes good" angle. I was proud of myself. Returning to my home town in actual show business was a self-satisfying feeling. However, soon it was time to return to New York and look for another job. I had no more ambition than to land another job in the chorus of a professional production, but I, of course, harbored hopes I could get into a show that was actually playing on Broadway.

Everyone in show business, except for Meryl Streep, is out of work from time to time and it is always scary. I began attending dance classes again to stay in shape and looked for auditions in the paper. A few months passed and I received a call from one of the male dancers who had been in *Zorba* with me. His name was Spencer Henderson.

"Rita, I got into *Promises, Promises*."

"Wow, that's great!"

"One of the dancers is leaving and they are having auditions tomorrow at two. Can you get here?"

One of my rules of show business is, "Opportunities don't wait for you to be ready. You have to be ready for the opportunity." Do you like that saying? I think I just made it up. Anyway, I had been diligent about attending various dance classes. I auditioned and got the job. I began rehearsals the following week and at the end of the month I was in my first Broadway show.

Promises, Promises is based on the 1960 film *The Apartment*, directed by Billy Wilder and starring Jack Lemmon and Shirley MacLaine. The songs were written by Burt Bacharach and Hal

David, and the book (theater jargon for the dialogue in between the songs) was by Neil Simon. The plot revolves around a junior executive at an insurance firm who allows company bosses to use his apartment to conduct affairs in return for corporate advancement.

Very often things you dream about aren't what they are cracked up to be. This wasn't one of those things. It was even better than I imagined. It was such a feeling of achievement. Whenever I opened that stage door and signed the call sheet, I really felt like I belonged. I had begun dancing lessons at the age of four and by the time I was seventeen, I was actually ON BROADWAY. Seventeen Magazine even did an article about me.

Okay, there were a few hiccups. The first night I appeared on stage, I didn't secure my hair on correctly, and Michael Bennett's choreography demanded multiple jerky head movements. I danced the "Turkey Lurkey Time" number on top of a desk holding on to my hair. At least I didn't fall off the desk. Well, not that night. In the "Grapes of Roth" dance, which took place in a singles bar, I was required to take a puff of a cigarette and put it out in another dancer's drink. It was an important action because it was the last moment in the number. I had never smoked a cigarette. The first few nights I added coughing to the routine.

The girls' dressing room had a welcoming atmosphere. Most of the chorus had been in the show for years. There were plants growing under grow lights and climbing up the make-up mirrors, while photos of family and loved ones adorned the dressing tables. When a chorus member is lucky enough to be a part of a long running show, his or her dressing room truly becomes a home away from home. On matinee days, when you perform a 2:00 p.m. show and an 8:00 p.m. show, you will be there for 10 hours. Yes, there is time to go out and eat between performances, but the fact that you have that 8:00 p.m. show in your future prohibits indulging in a big meal. The only time my fellow performers and I broke our no-big-meal-between-shows rule was on Thanksgiving. After the

Thanksgiving Day matinee, everyone went to Sardi's across the street for our turkey dinner. That evening, we all moved a little slower and jumped a little lower. Try to avoid seeing a show on Thanksgiving night.

Very soon after I joined *Promises, Promises,* a new actress was employed to play the lead. The production had been running for years and was no longer the must-see musical on Broadway. David Merrick, the producer, was a master at re-inventing shows and garnering publicity. Enter Lorna Luft; a terrific singer in her own right, she was also the half-sister of Liza Minnelli and the daughter of Judy Garland. The show received a media boost and ran for another few months. One night, I remember Lorna sticking her head into the girls' dressing room and saying, "Uncle Frank and Aunt Shirley are coming tonight." "Uncle Frank and Aunt Shirley" turned out to be Frank Sinatra and Shirley MacLaine.

The week between Christmas and New Year's Eve is the busiest period for Broadway shows. That's the peak of the tourist season and even the worst-attended shows are usually sold out. I, of course, was unaware of that fact and couldn't understand why a show that was selling out the previous week would close on January 2nd. I was once again unemployed. Our apartment lease was up and Jeanette had decided to move back home. I had saved enough money to rent a studio apartment on Broadway and 72nd Street. It was an L-shaped studio which meant it had an alcove for a bed. It did have a view…of the traffic. It was my first time living alone. I never felt lonely, though, because New York City always has so much going on. I took advantage of the museums, the film festivals, the restaurants, Bloomingdales and the half- price ticket booth for shows. Agatha and I had to switch our walks from Central Park to Riverside Park. She approved, even though the wind coming off the Hudson was unbelievably cold in the winter. I went back to dance class, adding acting and singing lessons into the mix to broaden my skill-set, and tried to get another job.

I do love being in show business, but you travel constantly. I'm always in hotels. I was staying in this Howard Johnson's once.... Their slogan used to be, and I'm not making this up, "If it's not your mother, then it must be Howard Johnson's." That was their slogan. I called down for room service at about four in the afternoon. I was hungry. They said, "No, it'll spoil your dinner." The maid came in every morning and said, "Clean up your room." As I was checking out, the lady behind the desk said, "Go ahead. Leave. Doesn't matter, I'll be dead in a couple weeks."

Four

One of my friends had a saying that I repeat to myself to this day: "Activity begets activity." I love that saying, even though I'm not entirely sure that "begets" is a word. Nothing happens if you stay in your apartment and wait for the phone to ring. I've found that, for me, doing something makes me much happier than waiting for someone to allow me to do something. Equity Library Theatre was holding auditions for *Carousel*. Equity Library Theatre was a non-profit theatre on 103rd Street and Riverside that mounted shows for out of work performers. The actors worked for free, as did all the backstage staff. I played a character named Armony. I had no speaking lines but I did have one solo singing line. I sang, "This was a real fine clambake."

During that production, I learned something else that has stuck with me. I had a friend in the cast named Zeke. He once mentioned that, whenever he went on stage, he always liked to "feel his feet on the floor." He said it made him feel grounded and in the moment. Even now, when I'm doing stand-up. I always try to feel my feet on the floor. It's excellent advice, unless you are an acrobat.

After *Carousel* closed, the showbiz papers told me there was a chorus audition for the hottest show on Broadway - *Follies*. You probably don't know this, and there's no reason why you should, but *Follies* was *the* show to be in on Broadway that year. I passed the first audition and was awarded with a callback. At the final audition, Michael Bennett was there, as was Hal Prince, as was the musical director of *Zorba*, Paul Gemignani. I got the job. I was dancing and singing in the chorus of the hottest show on Broadway.

With music and lyrics by Stephen Sondheim, *Follies* is about a reunion of past performers from a theatrical revue. It takes place in a Broadway theatre that's fallen into ruin and is now scheduled for demolition. The middle-aged protagonists are Buddy and Sally Durant Plummer and Benjamin and Phyllis Rogers Stone, two couples who attend the reunion. Sally and Phyllis were showgirls in the Follies during their youth. Several of the former showgirls perform their old numbers, sometimes accompanied by the ghosts of their former selves.

The *Follies* girls were not quite as friendly as the dancers in previous shows had been to me. I was the first replacement (i.e. not in the original cast) in the show and they were slow to accept me. There was one dancer, however, who made me feel very welcomed – Julie Pars, who is still, 50 years later, one of my very closest friends. I had no family in New York City except for my cousin Arlene, with whom I had little in common, so I latched on to Julie's family as if it were my own.

Unpacking my make-up and settling into my place in the dressing room, I noticed a bottle of white liquid on the table, accompanied by a sponge.

"What's this?" I asked Julie.

"Oh, that's the white body make-up you have to put on," she replied.

"For every show?"

"Yes. Then you have to take it off for the second act."

I thought the ghost effect was done with lighting. I was wrong. This was also my first experience dancing on a raked stage. A raked stage is a floor that slants and plays havoc with your balance. It took my equilibrium some time to become accustomed to it.

The *Follies* chorus was a mixture of showgirls and dancer/singers. The showgirls had to be over six feet and wore head dresses and platform shoes which ended up making them more than eight feet tall. They were also painted white and represented the ghosts of showgirls of the past. They strolled around slowly, arms out to the side, trying to keep their balance. Backstage in *Follies* was like being on Mars.

The white body make-up and the raked stage weren't my only problems. The girl I was replacing from the original cast was relatively flat-chested. I wasn't. I mentioned this to the wardrobe mistress and she said she didn't think it would be a problem. One night, while in a freeze pose in the tango, I noticed something was out of place. It was my left breast. I then heard giggling in the wings. I whispered to my partner, Kenny, "What should I do?"

"On the count of eight, I'll try to push it back in," he replied. As I exited into the wings the stage manager said, "Rita, you're a very exciting performer!" Kenny showed up years later when I was appearing at New York-New York in Las Vegas. We laughed about my unwanted exposure. Back then, it wasn't so funny. Okay, it was a little bit funny.

My father and Dagny came to New York to see me in the show. They weren't impressed. My dad said, "I couldn't even find you most of the time. Try to get in the front more." To be fair, I think he was proud of me. Broadway shows just weren't his thing. I don't remember Dagny saying anything. She considered the trip to New York a vacation for the two of them, rather than a visit involving me. One night, I remember crying about something, probably my mother, and Dagny said, "You know, this is our vacation. You can cry on your own time." I think it's good that she didn't adopt a child.

Follies was nominated for multiple Tony Awards. I had never been in a show that was nominated before. The night of the Tony's broadcast a few of us gathered together to watch the event. *Follies* won Best Score, Best Choreography, Best Scenic Design and Best Direction. Then it was time for Best Musical. We all agreed *Follies* was a sure thing. Drum roll please, brrrrrrrrrrump, Best Musical: *Two Gentleman of Verona.*

"Huh?" we all exclaimed. "How can we be the best in almost every category and not be Best Musical?"

The answer was, drum roll please, brrrrrrrrrrrump, there is no answer. Things happen in life and in show business that defy reason.

I think it was then that I became stoic regarding awards. I have to be honest, it's more fun to be nominated than not, and it's more fun to win than to lose, but it is one of those things that is out of your control. My attitude is that as long as I feel I've done my best, I'm satisfied.

Follies, although a critical hit, was not a commercial success. The producers decided they would close it on Broadway and would bring the cast to Los Angeles. I didn't want to go to Los Angeles. I had an agent, an apartment and a dog in New York and, most of all, I didn't know how to drive. Thanks to my father, I was petrified of learning. Michael Bennett wasn't happy. He called me aside one night after the show and said, "If you don't go to Los Angeles, you'll never work for me again."

I said, "I'm sorry you feel like that. I don't want to go to Los Angeles." I can't believe that at 18 I said "no" to one of the premier talents ever to work on Broadway. But I did. The cast went to Los Angeles largely intact. I stayed in New York. I was out of work again.

In between jobs on Broadway, I earned money performing in commercials, summer stock and industrial shows. Industrial shows are live shows about products. I sang and danced about cars, clothes, banks, clocks, cheese, whatever. Although I was never in *A Chorus Line* because of my altercation with Michael Bennett, I was hired by Marvin Hamlisch to sing songs from *A Chorus Line* when he performed his headlining live shows. Marvin played the piano in front of symphony orchestras and I sang "I Feel Nothing," plus had the high note in "At the Ballet," which scared me to death every time it rolled around. One evening, I think it was in Pittsburgh, I was waiting in the lobby for Marvin, along with my two friends who were singing the other songs. It was past the time we were supposed to leave for the theater. We waited and waited and finally called up to Marvin's room and there was no answer. An ambulance appeared at the front door of the hotel and emergency personnel hurried past us with medical equipment. We feared the worst. A few minutes later, the elevator door opened and Marvin appeared on a stretcher as the workers carried him through the lobby. He waved at the three of us, smiling as he was whisked by, and said, "Show canceled tonight, girls. Kidney stones." We got paid, had a delicious dinner in Pittsburgh and I didn't even have to hit the high note.

I auditioned for many shows that had no interest in hiring me. I can't remember them all, but I do recall that my focus, intensity and emotional investment in those auditions were so great that afterwards I would always go home and fall asleep for at least two hours. Broadway shows were few and far between. Each one took on an abnormal degree of importance. The auditions for *Mack and Mabel* were the talk of New York. It was obviously going to be an enormously prestigious production. David Merrick, Gower Champion and Jerry Herman were all powerhouse names. Although I had danced in two Broadway shows, this might be an opportunity to experience being part of one from its inception. It took three extremely long auditions to get that job as one of the 16 Mack Sennett bathing beauties. The final audition was in April. I went into the theater at 10:00 in the morning and the sun was shining. I danced. I sang. By the time I came out in the afternoon, it was snowing.

Mack and Mabel planned to go on the road for at least six months before coming to Broadway. I couldn't do that to Agatha. I decided to take a trip home and leave her with my father and Dagny. By that time, Tiny was 14. Agatha, on the other hand, was a frisky five-year-old. When I brought Agatha into the house, Tiny just stared at her like she was an irritating relative. "Oh my God! Not her!" Agatha again assumed the play position. Tiny again turned and slowly walked away. Like Dagny and me, they tolerated each other.

Starting a Broadway show from scratch was fascinating. Listening to the songs being sung for the first time, seeing the sets come to life and watching the dances get staged is an experience I'll never forget. Robert Preston was the star of the show, along with Bernadette Peters. Every day on the road we worked on something new and at night it would be put into the show. Sometimes it worked, sometimes it didn't.

Gower Champion had an idea for what was called the "fire sequence." Because the show was set in the time of silent films, he thought the "fire sequence" should be expanded to resemble a silent movie. He ordered a new orchestration and choreographed an entire silent film ballet. The new segment was added and it stopped the show, but in a bad way. It didn't move the plot forward and what was in Gower's head could not be achieved on stage. During intermission, Gower walked up and down the backstage halls saying, "Does anyone want to buy a very expensive fire sequence orchestration?"

During rehearsals, if the dancers were not in the section of the show being rehearsed, we had to wait in the hall. When Gower was creating a new routine, he would come out into the hall and call certain dancers into the studio. All of us always looked at him anxiously when the door to the rehearsal room opened. Sometimes I was chosen and sometimes I wasn't. It was a stressful but fair way to choose dancers. I feel I was extremely fortunate to get the chance to work for him.

We were in Washington D.C. when the producer, David Merrick, came to see the state of the production. He decided there needed to be a moment in the show that was more up-beat. He had produced Jerry Herman's *Hello Dolly* and he thought this show, by contrast, was depressing. It was about an abusive relationship between director Mack Sennett and silent movie star Mabel Normand and Mabel ends up dying of a drug overdose. I think it might have been the first "feel bad musical" so he had a point, but that was the story he had signed on to produce. David Merrick ordered new, extravagant costumes and told Gower Champion to choreograph something fun for the end of the first act. Mr. Champion didn't agree, but obliged. About a month later, the costumes arrived. They were long dresses in beautiful colors. Each dress was adorned with a matching, over-the-top hat. The dance went into the end of the first act. We waltzed around the stage. The dance ended. The audience was stunned. They didn't know who we were or why we were dancing. Instead of applauding, they just sat there. We never performed the dance again. David Merrick insisted that Gower Champion find somewhere in the show to wear the expensive costumes. We wore them for the curtain call.

Merrick didn't give up in his attempt to inject happiness into an unhappy story. *Hello, Dolly* had been a huge hit for the same team, and Merrick felt there needed to be an upbeat song for Mabel, played by Bernadette Peters. Jerry Herman, who is one of the nicest, most talented composers in the entire world, came up with "When Mabel Comes into the Room." The cast called the song "Hello Mabel." Mabel appeared on the second level balcony and entered the number by sliding down a fire pole. This proved extremely popular with the audience. I didn't personally know Robert Preston, but I do know that on the second night, he also slid down the pole. You don't become a star by accident.

The opening night on Broadway was ridiculously exciting. The audience loved the show and we received an enthusiastic standing ovation.

"We're in a hit! We're in a hit," I heard people say. The whole cast waited for the reviews at the top of one of those hotels that has big glass windows overlooking Manhattan. I had recently turned 21 and even drank a glass of champagne. Happy chatter was everywhere. Then came the reviews. Mixed. Decidedly mixed. Some papers loved it, some liked it, but the *New York Times*, the paper that mattered, was, "Eh." All that work, love and talent and, "Eh"? The air was quickly sucked out of our exhilaration balloon and slowly people began to drift out of the party.

Perhaps David Merrick had been right about the show needing to be more upbeat. *Mack and Mabel* never set the box office on fire and we only ran for a few months. *The Wiz* was receiving fabulous reviews out of town and was looking for a theater. Sadly, we came to work one day and saw the closing notice on the sign-in board. Ironically, just like *Follies*, *Mack and Mabel* has since become an iconic show that has been revived multiple times and is considered a classic. So much for "Eh."

After the show closed, I finally had time to return home to Miami to pick up Agatha. I didn't stay long. The first night I was there, my step-mother fed Tiny and left Agatha standing alone.

"Are you going to feed Agatha?" I asked.

"You feed her. She's your dog," Dagny replied.

"Okay, but I've been gone for a year. Has she not eaten? I figured they got fed together. Where do you keep her food?"

Dagny pointed to the pantry.

I fed Agatha. Obviously, I wasn't the only one not wanted on the voyage; Agatha wasn't allowed in the boat either.

Agatha and I returned to our studio apartment in New York. That evening it was time for her walk. I called her. She didn't come. I tried again. Nothing. I turned on the electric can opener in the kitchen. That was her favorite sound. She still did not appear. I looked everywhere and there aren't a lot of places to look in a studio apartment. How could I lose a 60-pound dog in a single room? I looked down the hall. Not there. Finally, I looked under my bed. There she was. Something was weird. She never went under my bed. Agatha saw me and finally crawled out. I said, "Do you want to go walkies?" She just stared at me. I grabbed her leash and Agatha came to the door. I figured it out. Agatha couldn't hear. The plane trip had been too hard on her sensitive dog ears. By the next morning she was back to responding, but I was happy I had made the decision not to take her on the "M&M" tour.

Not long after I returned to New York, I received the phone call that Tiny had died. My dad described Tiny looking up at him and wagging her tail one last time. Tiny had been a protector, a friend and a confidant. When any member of my family looked into her deep brown eyes, all we could see was complete devotion.

Why are women wearing perfumes that smell like flowers to attract men? Men don't like flowers. I've been wearing a great scent, though. It's called "New Car Interior."

You know how I end relationships now? I don't say, "This isn't working out" or "I don't want to see you anymore." If I never want to see a man again, I say, "You know, I love you. I want to marry you. I want to have your children." Sometimes they leave skid-marks.

Five

The lease was up for my studio apartment and I decided to take the dangerous leap that some New Yorkers take and some don't; I decided to rent an apartment with a bedroom. For the first time in my life, I had a view. I'd never had a view before and, if possible, I never want to live without one again. Every time I opened my apartment door I saw the magnificent George Washington Bridge. In daytime it was fantastic, but at night it was really spectacular, glittering like a diamond necklace in the sky. Dagny would like it! I could also see a portion of Central Park if I stuck my head out of the window and looked to the right. On New Year's Eve, I could see any aberrant fireworks that strayed from the pack.

My dad came up with a brilliant idea to bring Dagny and I closer together. He suggested she travel to New York and help me furnish my new apartment. I wasn't thrilled, but I knew nothing about decorating and certainly needed some help. As she arrived and was unpacking, I noticed that she had brought food in her suitcase. Not a jar of this or a package of that. She had brought a turkey. Not part of a turkey. A whole turkey. She had also brought a ham, salad, sweet potatoes and a few other items.

"Why did you bring all that food?" I asked.

"Because I didn't want to go into a dirty New York grocery store," she replied in her baby voice.

The first day of shopping was tense, but featured no major blow-ups. We bought a standing lamp and a glass dining room table with four chairs. The big disagreement came the following day. We purchased a sofa off the showroom floor that was to be delivered. When it arrived, Dagny and I argued about where to put it. I wanted to put it at the end of the living room and Dagny wanted to put it

46

against the wall. It was my apartment and the movers placed it at the end of the living room. After the delivery people left, Dagny locked herself in the bathroom. When she came out, the floodgates opened. She told me how unhappy she was in the marriage, how she hated going to work with my father and being his assistant in the office, how her life wasn't anything like she thought it was going to be, how he hadn't left her enough money in his will and how she was going to leave him when she returned to Miami. I was stunned. All I could say was, "I think you should maybe take these problems up with him."

"I will," she replied.

The next day she flew back to New York. I called my father the minute the door to my apartment closed behind her. I told him what she said and to be prepared when he met her at the airport.

The next day I heard nothing. The following day, nothing again. Finally, I called.

"What happened?" I asked.

"She never mentioned a thing. I don't know what you were talking about. Everything is fine. Gotta go. She's making me a martini."

I still don't know what to make of it, her, him, any of it. Relationships, you gotta love 'em.

Speaking of relationships, mine weren't going all that well either. I'm going to call all of my boyfriends "Brad" to avoid any legal ramifications. My first "Brad" was a fine, upstanding man whom I discovered was engaged to be married to someone else the whole time he was seeing me.

"Brad Two" was a lot better. We dated on and off for about three years. We were both in love. I with him and he with his car. He had an antique Jaguar convertible that was more unreliable than Judy Garland. We could only frequent restaurants that had a parking space in front so he could watch his car while we ate. Once, when I turned up to his apartment, the brakes to his car were in his sink. Ten years later, that ended up as a joke in my act.

When I went on the road for a few months with *Mack and Mabel*, I asked Brad Two to water the plants in my apartment. Since B2 wasn't particularly a plant person, I took him over to my apartment and pointed them out to him. When I returned a few months later, all of my plants were in fine condition except for one.

"What happened to this one?" I asked.

"You didn't point to that one," he replied.

"Yes, I did!"

"No, you didn't."

"You thought I wanted that plant to die?" I asked incredulously.

"I wondered why you didn't point to it."

I told you B2 wasn't a plant person.

I can't remember what our real issues were. I only know that we were both in our early twenties and so weren't yet capable of figuring ourselves out, let alone another person. He lived in the high-rise across the street and our apartments looked into each other. I wasn't in a show at the time of our final break up and the temptation to look across to see what was going on in his apartment was intense. I guess this was an early version of stalking an ex on social media. I had to do something to get myself out at night. I'd always wanted to learn how to play tennis and heard about a night-time tennis clinic over on the east side. Charlene was in town for a while (she was now a principal dancer with the Joffrey Ballet Company and travelled quite a bit), so we decided to go together.

I wasn't a tennis natural. My hand-eye coordination consisted of being able to hit myself in the eye with my hand. However, I loved it. This well-meaning, innocent endeavor led to an extremely dangerous moment in my life. Playing tennis in New York City is not easy. My Sunday mornings began by bicycling to the courts in Central Park at 7:00 in the morning. There, I would meet my partner and we would get in a line to sign up for a court for a few hours later in the day. Usually, I cycled back home, read the Sunday Times and cycled back for my 11:00 a.m. reservation. This particular Sunday, my partner decided to go back home and I decided to stay and wait, instead of bicycling back and forth. While I was waiting, I thought, "Why not warm up by jogging around the reservoir?" It was a beautiful Sunday morning and, although it wasn't crowded, there were other joggers running around the track, except for the moment a man jumped out of the bushes, grabbed me around the neck from behind and ordered me not to scream. He tried to drag me into the bushes. Fortunately, I had the presence of mind to scream at the top of my lungs and the man disappeared. Other joggers eventually came to my aid and escorted me back to the courts to call the police (no cell phones then.) I rode in a police car back to the station and was shown various pictures of suspects. None of them resembled my attacker. I can still see his face in my mind to this day and I realize that I was very lucky. I also have a very good reason for why I don't jog.

I was working more and more, and having to put Agatha in a kennel when I was out of town because I didn't want her to fly. Two things were coming together: I couldn't be home enough for Agatha and my dad was now without a dog in the house in Miami. I put Agatha in her giant crate and flew her one more time down to Miami. As I told you before, dogs brought out the best in my father. He loved Agatha as much as he loved Tiny and was much happier the next time we talked on the phone. I'm not sure how Dagny felt about having my dog in her house, so I made sure to put my father in charge of feeding her.

It was a busy time for me in New York. I had just booked an industrial show for TWA. For those of you who don't remember, TWA was an airline that went out of business in the 1980s. This was a dream job that involved going to London for three weeks to perform the show. We rehearsed in a theatre in the West End and Peter Sellers was the star. TWA paid Peter a hefty sum to star in a new campaign for the airline in which he would create quirky characters and perform monologues. I was one of four singer/dancers hired to perform musical numbers in between his quirkiness.

A few problems arose. Peter was not a people person. He was extremely pleasant when we went to his dressing room to introduce ourselves, but he never said a word to any of us after that initial meeting. He also wasn't used to performing live, and the TWA executives who had been flown in from all over the world couldn't hear anything he said from the stage. To add to the problem, when the commercials aired on television, Peter's characters were so complete that nobody knew it was Peter Sellers. His famous character in America was Inspector Clouseau from the Pink Panther films. Due to his movie contract, that was the one character he was forbidden to portray.

You'll notice I'm not mentioning any of the auditions for shows I didn't get. That's because there are so many of them they have morphed into one big land-fill of rejection. Rejection is something every performer goes through…. except, of course, Meryl Streep. The choreographer I always wanted to work for was Bob Fosse. He would never hire me. I attended his auditions in low-cut leotards, boots, false eyelashes and false other things. No matter how hard I tried to look like a Bob Fosse dancer, he saw right through it and I was always cut: if not right away, soon after right away.

The auditions for the musical *Pippin,* directed by Fosse, were held while I was in *Follies.* I went to the audition with another dancer in the show named Jennifer Nairn Smith. Jennifer was one of the most stunning-looking women I had ever met. She often arrived in our backstage dressing room wearing a fur coat with nothing on underneath. She was six feet tall and almost all legs. Standing next to JNS at an audition was like standing next to the Empire State Building. I did my best to look sexy, but when Jennifer took off her coat, she revealed a crocheted leotard that emphasized every one of her bountiful assets. On leaving the audition, we were stopped and asked to leave a phone number where we could be reached. Jennifer was coming over to my apartment, so we left my number. By the time we arrived the phone was ringing. I ran excitedly to answer it. The voice on the other end said, "We are looking for Jennifer Nairn Smith." I handed JNS the phone. She was in the show. I fooled nobody with my false everythings.

Luckily, there were choreographers who would hire me. After *Mack and Mabel,* I was in the chorus of a show called *So Long 174th Street.* The next step after dancing and singing in the chorus is to have an actual part. You've no doubt read a theater program while waiting for a musical to start. I was still listed in the clutch of performers at the end of the program, grouped together as the chorus. However, although I still didn't have a part in this show, I did have a line. In the middle of a dance I had to stand and point at the star of the show, Robert Morse, and yell, "Look! It's David Kolowitz, the actor!" I did it to the best of my ability, but the show closed in a month. My fault.

The Magic Show was running on Broadway and needed a standby for two of the leads in the show. The difference between a "standby" and an "understudy" is that an understudy has to be at the theater every night. A standby just has to call into the theater and make sure everyone is well and ready to roll. It's a great job, except for when you get the call and you're in your pajamas, watching a really good movie, there is a major snow storm, no buses and you have to walk to the theater. That's what happened to me one snowy evening. I was watching an old Bob Hope movie when my phone rang.

Herb, the stage manager, said, "Natalie's sick. She isn't going to be in tonight. You're on as Charmin."

"Why are you having a show?" I asked. "It's snowing and there are no buses running."

"The producers don't want to cancel."

My apartment was on 64th Street and the theater was on 47th Street. There was no subway line that could take me close to my destination, so I ran in the snow. The cast and I performed to around 20 wet, frozen people in the audience. Call me suspicious, but I don't think Natalie was really sick that evening.

I learned things in *The Magic Show* that were never taught to me in ballet class. I was sawn in half and transformed into a tiger. I signed a form that prohibits me from disclosing how the illusions are achieved, but I'm sure they are now somewhere on the internet being performed by someone who is naked. I can divulge that the tiger's cage I had to wait in smelled really bad.

That year I received a call from my father that Dagny had finally left him and was filing for divorce. I didn't know what to say, except that I thought they would both be better off. That's not where the saga ended, however. About a month after she left, Dagny was diagnosed with breast cancer and came back to my father. Although he still hadn't purchased health insurance, he took her back and paid for her medical expenses. My dad wasn't perfect, but when his wives needed him, he was there. Thankfully for Dagny, it was months rather than years before she passed away. After Dagny died, my dad and I became much closer. I was able to call him whenever I wanted and to visit him and Agatha a few times a year without fear of causing mayhem in Miami, which is a good title for something.

In between jobs, I was continuing to take acting lessons as well as dancing and singing. Not only did these lessons keep me in performing shape, they also prepared me for what I saw as my next step on the Broadway ladder: graduating from the chorus and performing a principal part.

I tried many different acting teachers before I found a style to which I could relate. Even if I was completely lost by what was going on in some of my acting classes, I found there were always a few things I could take away from each teacher that were beneficial.

At the Lee Strasburg Institute, sense memory was an important exercise. I spent hours trying to recreate holding an imaginary mug of hot coffee and then pretending to drink it. From practicing those exercises, I learned concentration and discovered that after pretending to drink a cup of coffee, I needed a cup of coffee.

My next acting teacher was a man named Warren Roberson. His teaching style was completely different. A student would stand on stage, recreate a harrowing event in their life and invariably end up crying hysterically. I signed up for a month's worth of lessons and never once volunteered to go on stage. Something inside told me I wasn't ready to recreate my mother's death in front of the class. Although I never participated, it was beneficial to know that a technique in acting was to call on events in your past to influence your on-stage emotions.

Mary Tarcai, was an eccentric woman who taught in a more practical style. In her studio we learned monologues and scenes. She sometimes handed us passages from plays and had us perform them on the spot. The valuable lesson I learned from Mary Tarcai was, "Think about what you're saying and pick up your cues." If you never attend an acting class and find yourself appearing in a play or movie, just remember those two things and you will be halfway there.

Stella Adler's acting studio was enlightening. Her philosophy was to use your imagination to get to an emotion. One of my favorite bits of advice she gave was when we were wandering around the class impersonating different animals. She said, "Don't pretend you're the duck. Be the duck."

I also studied with Wynn Handman, who was one of the most encouraging teachers I've ever had. However, studying with Larry Moss was when things I had learned with previous teachers actually came together. I knew Larry from *So Long 174th Street*. I heard he was teaching acting and decided to give it another try. Timing is so important in both relationships and career. In my late twenties I was ready to be less self-aware and more committed to being the duck. Larry's technique involved examining the text and creating a character from clues in the writing. He later moved to Hollywood and is still one of the top acting coaches working today.

Keep in mind, I didn't attend all of these different drama classes consecutively. This was over a period of ten years. Acting was never my strong point, but I feel it informed my comedy, writing and stage presence. I figured anything I learned could only help!

My next and last show on Broadway was *Annie* in 1979. I played Lily St. Regis, one of the show's leading principals. This was a really big deal to me. This was the first part I had where I didn't have to wait for someone to get sick before I was allowed to speak on stage. I had to play a dumb blonde. For the audition, I used a thick, high-pitched New York accent and when I heard laughter coming from the dark theater, I knew I had a chance. I was home watching television when my phone rang and I received the news that I had the role. I actually put the phone to my chest and screamed. After ten years, I actually had a part on Broadway. I played Lily St. Regis for a year. People sometimes asked me, "How do you play the same part for a year? Isn't it boring?" The answer is that, for me, it was never boring. I could always find something - an inflection, a nuance, or a reaction - that kept me interested.

I was 27 and had been working in musicals for 11 years. I can't really pin-point why I decided to try a new direction. I still loved show business, but the wide-eyed enthusiasm I'd felt at 16 had morphed into weariness at the auditioning process. Contemporaries were becoming choreographers, trying different career paths and/or starting families. I wasn't sure I had the talent or drive to compete for the handful of juicy female roles on offer each Broadway season, nor did I particularly want to return to the chorus.

I read the New York Times pretty thoroughly most days, trying to get a perspective on the world, the arts, and business news. One day I read an article about a new product that had been introduced into the marketplace. *Soft soap*. It was a colossal success. The article explained that when introducing a new product into the market place, you had to be either better or different. A new bar soap would have to be better than all existing soaps to find a niche in a crowded market place. A new, different type of soap product would have its own market.

I then thought of the thousands of female dancers, actresses and singers in show business, of which I was one. However, when I thought of female comedians, there were only a handful. I figured, why not try that? Even though I was getting laughs in *Annie*, none of my friends ever thought I was particularly amusing. They were always funnier than me. I was never the class clown. I never really even talked much. Dancer to comedian; you'll agree it's not a natural progression. You don't become a dancer because you're verbal and you don't become a comedian because you're light on your feet. All I can tell you is that it made sense to me. I'm not saying that I'm a late bloomer, but most people begin talking when they are two. I began talking when I was 27.

One night, after a performance of *Annie*, I walked to the Improv, a tiny comedy club between Eighth and Ninth Avenues. I asked one of the comedians how much five minutes of comedy material would cost. He said, "About $3,000." That's when I decided to learn how to write jokes. I found out that auditions were held at the Improv for new comedians one day a month. I began writing thoughts in a note book to prepare for my comedy debut. On the day specified, I arrived at around 2:00 in the afternoon. There was already a line of auditionees on the sidewalk. Some had lounge chairs, some had blankets with pillows; I just had my pants. I sat on the sidewalk with my note book and tried to work on my set. A few hours later, someone from the club came and counted 12 people down the line that would be allowed to audition that night. I was number 13. So much for my first foray into stand-up comedy.

A friend of mine in the cast of *Annie*, Richard Walker, always wanted to try comedy and he suggested we try a double-act. Richard was a terrific singer and he proposeed that we sing a song and pause intermittently to tell jokes. That way, if the jokes weren't funny, we could start singing right away and maybe people wouldn't notice. I didn't want to wait another month to audition, so I found out there was another comedy club on the East Side, Catch a Rising Star, that had auditions weekly. The auditions were on a Monday night, when *Annie* was dark, so it was all working out perfectly. Richard and I hired a pianist and practiced our song and joke combo in preparation for our big night. I had heard that people began lining up very early in the morning to get an audition number at Catch. Richard and I agreed to meet at 8:00 in the morning. When we arrived, we were number eight. There were only ten numbers passed out that morning so Richard and I were in.

"What time do you think we'll get on?" I asked the number-giver.

"Be here by 8:00," he replied perfunctorily.

Richard and I practiced during the day and met at the club at eight on the dot, figuring we would be on by 8.30 at the latest. We sat in the bar for hours before it was our turn. By the time we got on stage, it was 1:00 a.m. and there were three people in the audience. Richard turned to me during our set and said through gritted teeth, "I never want to do this again." I did.

I was on Broadway last year in Annie. *I played the prostitute. A few years earlier I was in* The Magic Show. *I played the prostitute. I don't know why I'm always playing prostitutes. In high school, I was voted the girl most likely to become a nun. That may not be very impressive to you now, but it was quite an accomplishment at the Hebrew Academy.*

Six

So, if I wanted to be a comedian, the big question I had to ask myself was, why would anyone laugh when I stopped talking? I had no idea. The quips that Richard and I wrote certainly weren't effective. I do recall one of my first attempts at humor that I wrote in my notebook was a monologue about being a trapeze artist with sweaty palms. It did create an image, but I wasn't a trapeze artist. I had failed the first test of comedy; I wasn't being honest.

I decided to work backwards. What made me laugh? Well, at the time I loved Woody Allen movies and I discovered he had recorded a stand-up album. I found it at the Lincoln Center Library and listened to it multiple times. His character and what he talked about meshed perfectly. One of my favorite jokes: "I'd like to say something positive, but I can't think of anything. Will you take two negatives?" If he was a nerdy, Jewish intellectual, who was I?

My first ambition was to think of one joke. Just one single joke. It couldn't be that hard. My friends were so important to me in that process. I would call them up and leave messages on their answering machines asking, "Is this funny?" My friend Julie was so encouraging. She always answered, "Not yet." My dressing roommate in *Annie*, a terrific singer named Mary Bracken Phillips, limited me to five tries a day. Sometimes I snuck in six. My first joke that worked was about being a single woman in New York and dating. It went like this, "My boyfriend and I broke up. He wanted to get married. I didn't want him to." Hmmmm. Sounds suspiciously like my first boyfriend who was engaged to someone else. Honest.

The Lincoln Center Library was a great source of comedic information. I read, Freud's *Analysis of Wit and Humor* but I didn't find the humor in the book funny. I don't think it helped me much or maybe I was too stupid to understand what Sigmund was talking about. I kept reading and taking out comedy albums from the library, trying to learn what I could from them. A few things stuck. Mel Brooks said, "If you start from the truth, at least you have a place to start." That seemed like good advice. Staring at a blank piece of paper trying to write something funny can be quite intimidating.

The other thing I learned is that you never know where a joke is going to come from. I was reading a book called *The Making of a Psychiatrist*. What could be funny about that? Well, a blurb in the front of the book read, "Neurotics build castles in the air, Psychotics live in them." I finished the thought with, "My mother cleans them." I called up Julie immediately. She didn't say, "Not yet." She laughed.

Across the street from where we performed *Annie* was a bar called Ye Old Triple Inn. One night, as I was leaving the theater, I noticed a sign in the bar's window: *Thursday night is comedy night*. I finally had about three or four minutes of material about growing up as an only child in Miami and decided to give it a try. It wasn't the most glamorous bar in the world, but it had two huge plusses. It was across the street from the theater and I didn't have to sit on the sidewalk for ten hours.

The stage was tiny and, as if I wasn't scared enough, there was a dart board on one side being used by customers who had been drinking. The bar's attempt at a comedy night hadn't caught on yet, so only three of us were prepared to perform. There weren't many people in the bar and the people who were present weren't there for the comedy, so the first two potential comedians went on stage and nobody paid much attention to them. However, nobody was hit by a dart, so that was promising. When it was my turn, I said my few jokes and actually got some chuckles. I couldn't tell if they were laughing at me or my jokes or each other, but I did my three minutes and the manager said I could come back any time and that would be a dollar for my Diet Coke. I said, "I'll see you next Thursday."

The next time I sat on the sidewalk at the *Improv*, I made sure to bring a pillow and arrive early. I was given a number and was on stage before midnight. I can't remember my first comedy set, but I do remember being heckled. Someone in the audience said something original like, "You suck!" or "Get a job!" I didn't have a comeback, so I just said, "I'm sorry, but this is my first time on stage. Could you please come back and heckle me when I'm more experienced?" That put the audience on my side of the argument and the remainder of my set must have gone reasonably well because the manager of the club, Chris Albrecht, who later became a majorly influential executive in television, said I could come and hang out and watch comedians any time I wanted. So that's what I did. Every night after *Annie*, I went to the *Improv* and watched comedians. It was fascinating. Some nights the atmosphere was electric and some nights it was like sitting in a wet cardboard box. What I found extremely interesting was listening to the auditionees on Monday nights. The jokes they had written often didn't go over, but the patter while they were being themselves in between the jokes was amusing. What I had to figure out was how to both be myself and be amusing.

My problem was acquiring stage time. Although I was allowed to sit and listen to the comedians whenever I wanted, I was very rarely allowed on stage. When I was, it was usually 1:00 in the morning or later. Although the manager of the club thought I had potential, Silver, the owner, didn't. One evening she pulled me aside and said, "I don't like your voice. It's too soft. It's not a comedy voice. If you want me to put you on stage more, you're going to have to go to a speech coach."

In show business, as in any other line of work, people are going to give you advice. Some of it will be helpful, and some of it will be the opposite. I recall an agent from a prominent talent agency advising me to wear a big bow in my hair and a wedding dress and only talk about how much I wanted to get married. As appealing as that sounded, I decided to ignore that suggestion. With regards to changing my voice, I thought, the fact that I didn't sound like a comedian might be a plus. Rather than change my voice, I decided to change my locale.

A piano bar had recently opened up around the corner from the Improv. Comedians were welcomed. It was an intimate space that sat around fifty people at its maximum. The audiences were generally the after-theatre crowd, so heckling wasn't an issue. What was an issue was that the bar itself was located uncomfortably close to the stage and blended cocktails were the house specialties. Very often, just as I was about to reveal my punchline, the loud blender-whirling would interrupt. Although this was intrusive, it was also helpful in that it made me slow down, relax and be aware of my surroundings, instead of rushing through the lines I had memorized. Any negative situation can be a learning experience. I keep telling that to my daughter. I know she wishes I would stop.

Living in New York was a tremendous help in my quest to find the funny. Not only did it have the Lincoln Center Library, but the Museum of Broadcasting had recently opened as well. I remembered that my mother liked a comedian called Jack Benny. The Museum of Broadcasting had collected all the old Jack Benny television shows, and I sat there and watched these amazing shows that are still funny to this day. For me, Jack Benny had the most complete, natural comedic character that I had or have ever seen. He didn't look funny; he looked like a banker. He was under-stated and totally serious about everything he was saying and doing. Nothing he did seemed artificial or forced. These are qualities I'm still striving to attain. I also loved *The Burns and Allen Show*. Again, it was impossible to separate George and Gracie's characters from who they were in real life. The character of Gracie Allen, who was so sure she was right about subjects she was so wrong about, was and is timeless.

New York also had film festivals. Because I worked at night, Buster Keaton, Charlie Chaplin, Preston Sturges and Jacques Tati were just a few of the artists I discovered during the day. You're not going to understand this connection immediately, but don't worry; it will become slightly clearer in the near future. One of my comedy influences was Liberace (I warned you it wouldn't make sense right away.) I had a friend who was an ex-Rockette. Liberace was performing at Radio City Music Hall and my friend said we could get in for free. Well, free was, and is, my middle name. I wasn't a Liberace fan, but I thought seeing Liberace's show might be interesting. Also, have I mentioned it was free?

I sat in the uppermost section of Radio City Music Hall. A rhinestone-covered piano adorned with a huge candelabra sat center-stage. Liberace appeared in a smothering fur coat looking like a gay bear. He began to talk to the audience and suddenly I forgot that I was sitting in a seat so far up that I was accruing frequent flyer miles. In a venue that large, Liberace's connection was so intimate and personal, I felt he was talking to me. I understood that it wasn't his piano playing that made him so successful; it was his ability to connect with an audience. I made a mental note to put that in my arsenal of things to work on.

As with many things in life, stand-up comedy is about power. The person with the microphone possesses the power in the room. For most of the 20th century, men owned society's power, so a female stand-up was an uncomfortable concept to many. Adopting an aggressive persona made audiences more comfortable, as aggression is a more male trait. I simply couldn't do aggressive. I was quiet, unassuming and shy. I employed a softer manner, which in turn allowed me to conceal a sly, unexpected undertone. That's why I've always been drawn to writing concentrated material (I dislike the term "one liner" because that seems to me dismissive, as though being verbose is somehow easier than being precise). I like setting up something that appears mild and then delivers an unexpected conclusion containing a sting. The surprise of that formula produces the laugh reaction. The more powerful and surprising the punch of the punchline, the bigger the laugh. I also discovered that the surprise allowed me to disguise the power and transformed my shyness into an asset and an alternate to aggression.

Interestingly, most younger comedians take the aggressive route, as did my most successful contemporaries (Roseanne, Kathy Griffin and Rosie O'Donnell spring to mind). I suspect Sarah Silverman is the nearest to my style, although she adds a degree of raunchiness which suits the less censorious times. I still think men in power are more comfortable with an aggressive approach, and I'm reminded that it's powerful men who most often enjoy sexual submission and being dominated. I had a friend whose high-flying Manhattan lawyer husband waited until the first night of their marriage before asking her to smack him around.

One night, after performing a set at the piano bar, I was hanging around the Improv and actually got the chance to do a set before midnight. It went pretty well. Bill Maher came up to me and asked if I ever went to Catch a Rising Star. I said, "No." I felt it was wise to neglect to mention my first attempt with my friend, Richard.

"I'm the emcee on most nights," Bill continued. "Why don't you come over there? I'll see if I can put you on." I didn't need to be asked again. Catch became my new comedy home. The only drawback was that after performing in *Annie*, I had to take two buses to get there. On the plus side, that gave me more time to work on my act. Remember what I said about negatives? You want me to stop too, don't you? Come on, admit it.

From then on, I was a regular at Catch. Jerry Seinfeld, Bill Maher, Paul Reiser and Richard Belzer were already headliners at the club. I was able to observe and learn from a whole new set of comics. Gradually, I began to get stage time there before midnight. At this level of comedy, there was no money changing hands; only food. If you were able to do a set, you could choose between a hamburger or a spinach salad. I was still performing every night in *Annie* and sporadically booking commercials, so a spinach salad was fine with me.

Commercials were a wonderful income supplement to my *Annie* salary, but not great for my soul. Although I appeared in maybe 30 television ads, I auditioned for hundreds. I heard lots of casting people mumble to each other "not pretty enough," "too ethnic," "too old," etc. There were too many people who were better qualified for those jobs. I think I reached my limit when, at an audition, I had to pretend to take a shower while enjoying the smell of the imaginary soap (the hot coffee practice helped) and I heard a casting person say, "I don't like her arms."

One of the rules in my life I try to obey is this: if something you are doing is making you unhappy, stop doing it. Going on auditions for commercials was eating away at my self-confidence. In a looks contest, I was always going to lose. At least in comedy, if the people were laughing, they weren't judging my arms! I never went on another casting call for commercials. I waited until I was well known enough that advertising agencies specifically requested me.

When my contract with *Annie* was up, I realized I had no desire to audition for another Broadway show. My myopic personality was now totally focused on comedy, writing and performing my own material. It was the best decision I ever made. You are either a comedian or something else. There were a few comedians in the club who were lawyers or dentists during the day. That just doesn't work. Somehow the audience knows you're not committed. A comedian's day has to be about avoiding trying to write jokes while trying to write jokes. There was another female comedian at the club, Marjorie Gross. We made each other laugh so we decided to hang out during the day and try to write comedy together. Sometimes we gave up and went to the movies, but sometimes we came up with a premise or a punchline. You never know, you just have to try. As Woody Allen once said, "Ninety per cent of life is showing up."

Marjorie eventually became a successful comedy writer in Hollywood. We also bonded over our mother's deaths. Her mother died of ovarian cancer when she was young. Unfortunately, Marjorie died of ovarian cancer before she was 40. I still miss her.

The great thing about Catch was that another club, the Comic Strip was within walking distance. Plus, the Comedy Cellar had opened up in the Village. I could hit three clubs in one night. I began to book weekend spots that paid $15 for cab fare. A local booker, Jerry Stanley, was also offering a few $50 gigs in restaurants in New Jersey. Three comedians would be hired for each job: a headliner, a middle act and a comedian who had a car. I was the middle act.

You never knew what you were going to encounter with a Jerry Stanley gig. He never told you what the place would be like or how far away it was. The question comedians always asked when told a gig was 25 miles away was, "Regular miles or Jerry Stanley miles?"

These early performances were an adventure. A bit of advice gleaned from those days: don't play restaurants where they keep barrels of peanuts near the customers. One night, a few drunken patrons thought it would be appropriate to throw nuts at us during our show. Another bit of advice: try to find out if it is a regular audience or a theme night. Let me tell you what happened to me in a club in God Knows Where, New Jersey. I knew something was wrong when I got out of the car and had to pass a rooster fight in the parking lot. When I entered the club, it was evident that the clientele was made up exclusively of bikers. I later found out it was indeed "Hell's Angels' Night." What chance did I have of not being booed off the stage? The only thing I could think of in that situation was to be totally honest. I opened with, "I know this probably isn't going to go too well, so just laugh at the jokes you like and stare at me for the rest of them. This will be over in 20 minutes. So…. Have any of you ever been to the ballet?" There was a laugh and I quickly followed it with my sure-fire ballet joke: "I had to quit the ballet after I injured a groin muscle. It wasn't mine."

Finding a way into a set in a tricky situation can be challenging, but if you enter on the correct wavelength the audience will generally follow you wherever you go. "Hell's Angels' Night" wasn't one of my finer performances, but I didn't bomb either. All experiences have value. Not only can I write about them in this book, but they were all part of making me who I am as a comedian today.

I just broke up with my boyfriend. An awful thing about breaking up with someone is when they want to stay your friend. Why do they want to do that? Why can't they get lost? This one guy used to call me all the time. I'd say, "Look, I don't have anything to tell you." He'd say, "Just tell me the same things you tell your friends." So, I told him how horrible he was.

Seven

There were a few reasons comedy took off in the 1980s. One of them was *Late Night with David Letterman*. David Letterman's quirky style of humor spoke to comedians of my generation and he was our idol. He was irreverent, sarcastic, innovative and we all aspired to be on his show. Very often the person who booked the comedy segment, Bob Morton, would wander into Catch to watch comedians. There was always a nervous hum underneath the ambient chitter-chatter in the bar whenever Morty showed up. Who would get on? Who was he there to see? How was the crowd? All of a sudden, it wasn't just another night. It was a night that could get you on *Late Night with David Letterman*.

A manager saw me at one of the clubs, taped a short performance and sent it to Bob Morton. I had been at Catch for about a year, working diligently on my material. This was my mantra; it didn't matter where it was or what time it was, I had to talk into a microphone every single night. Some nights, when my set was at 1:00 or even later in the morning, I would go to sleep after setting my alarm for midnight, then get dressed, hail a cab and go tell jokes. Once, I remember having a set at a restaurant on Third Avenue at 1:00 a.m. When I arrived, the audience had all gone home. I did my set for the waitresses who were clearing the tables. They laughed, so it was all good.

When my time came to audition for Bob Morton, I was ready. The bad news was that my audition was on a Tuesday night. Audiences are usually not that good on Tuesdays. They get happier as you get closer to the weekend. The worse news was that it was raining. A Tuesday night audience in the rain was death. It meant there wouldn't be many people in the audience and the people who would be there would be wet. People don't laugh when they're wet. They chuckle.

My audition didn't go well. There are always circumstances you cannot control no matter how well prepared you are. I couldn't pick the day, I couldn't control the weather and I couldn't make that audience laugh. I did make them chuckle, but I knew that wasn't enough. I was devastated. When I got off-stage, Bob said, "I know it was a bad audience, but I like your persona and your material. Let's try again next week." Next week arrived and the same material worked perfectly. It was still a Tuesday, but it wasn't raining and the audience was attentive, alert and dry. I was booked on *Late Night with David Letterman* for the show on August 26th, 1982.

The day of the filming was unbelievably stressful. I adopted a technique that I still use to this day when I'm afraid to do something. I tell myself that if other people can do it, so can I. I then pretend to be confident. Nobody can tell whether you're pretending to be confident or if you really are confident. I knew other comedians who had been on the show. I hung around with them all the time. They were just regular people. I arrived at NBC studios and went into make-up. Make-up quickly became one of my favorite things about being on television; someone who knows how to make you look better than you normally look makes you better than you normally look. All you have to do is sit there and have a face.

I waited in my dressing room and rehearsed my set repeatedly. I was given five minutes of air time. My average was three jokes a minute. I left one minute for laughter, so my total was 12 jokes. About five minutes before my set Bob dropped by to wish me good luck and then added, "By the way, we're running a little bit long. Could you cut a minute?"

"Cut a minute"?! I went through my set. Everything was connected. I had an opening line and a closing joke that had to stay. I found three lines in the middle that could be eliminated and hoped

I wouldn't blank on national television. Waiting off-set, I heard David Letterman's announcement.

"This is her network television debut, so make her feel at home. Please welcome, Rita Rudner."

I found my mark, started talking and in four minutes it was over. I wasn't sure how it went, but people in the audience laughed and members of the TV crew said, "Good job." Walking back to my apartment, I re-lived my experience and tried to evaluate what had just happened. I didn't forget anything and I didn't fall over. However, I would have to wait until later that night to see what it really had looked like. The show taped in the late afternoon and I was home by six. I couldn't wait alone for seven hours, so at eight I was back at Catch. All of my comedian friends were asking me how it went and I told them the truth: I had no idea.

That night, or should I say the next morning, at 1.25 a.m., I saw myself on television saying thoughts that I had written myself. As a dancer, I was told how to move; as a singer I was told what note to sing; and as an actress I was told what to say. To be on television and to be in control of what I was saying and doing was a tremendously satisfying feeling. My first phone call was from my dad. He had stayed up to watch me. He said. "Keep doing that. I don't want to have to see any more Broadway shows." I knew that was his way of saying he was proud of me.

The next morning, I ventured out of my building to see if anyone recognized me. My doorman, Caesar, was the first to say, "Rita, I saw you on television last night. You were funny. When are you going to be on again?"

Then it dawned on me; that was my best five, I mean four, minutes. I had created my own product, but it only lasted 240 seconds. The pressure to write jokes became even more intense. When I was new in the clubs I once asked Jerry Seinfeld how he wrote jokes. He won't remember telling me this because I last talked to him a billion dollars ago, but he said, "It's my job. I just sit down and do it."

Success is never an accident. Jerry is very talented, but he's also tremendously disciplined and a hard worker. The art of writing isn't easy for anyone. People always ask me what my favorite joke is and I always tell them it's the one I haven't thought of yet.

So, David Letterman's show was certainly one of the reasons stand-up comedy prospered in the eighties, just as *The Ed Sullivan Show* had been a performing opportunity a few decades earlier. Another reason was the arrival of cable television. When cable television was in its infancy, the one thing its executives were looking for was cheap programming. What is cheaper than a comedian, a microphone and a brick wall? Filming a fish tank is the only thing I can think of. Cable television executives soon began swarming the clubs, looking for ever-eager comedians to showcase.

Rick Newman, the owner of Catch, recommended me for *The Catch A Rising Star 10th Anniversary Special* on HBO. It starred, Robin Williams, Billy Crystal, Richard Belzer, Pat Benatar, Gabe Kaplan, Andy Kaufman and me. I was given four minutes in the middle of the show and was introduced as "New Comedian Rita Rudner." It was a big break, made an even bigger break when one of the producers, Pat Lee, came into my trailer and said, "You're scheduled to go on after Andy Kaufman. I think we should sneak you on before he goes on. Andy always leaves the audience a little confused." Andy Kaufman's act was surreal. He took chances no one else would ever think of taking. For this special, he chose to have someone heckle him mercilessly from the audience. The crowd didn't know what to think. Was this really happening? Was it planned? One thing was sure; they were confused and it was a good thing I went on before him. Thank you, Pat.

I was working as a comedian more often and, except for a bad date here and there, wasn't very interested in romantic relationships. I hung around with male comedians quite a bit, but we were always getting together to write jokes. I was essentially one of the guys. Of course, eventually a Brad 3 showed up. I met him at the club. He was good-looking, smart, personable and it was another on and off situation for a while. Let's quote good ol' Maya Angelou: "When someone tells you who they are, believe them." A few months into the relationship, Brad 3 told me that he really liked me, but he wasn't interested in dating only one person. I've never understood going out with more than one person at a time, so I thought, "He's just saying that." He wasn't just saying that. Which turned out to be a good thing, because when someone showed up at Catch and asked me to perform at the Edinburgh Festival in Scotland, I said, "Yes, Scotland sounds far away and that is where I would like to be." The man producing the show turned out to be important.

Here is another rule I always attempt to follow: I try to say "yes" more than I say "no." I don't mean say "yes" to stupidly dangerous things like drugs or racquet ball, but say "yes" to career opportunities that might sound scary or might not seem perfect at the time. There are enough people in the world who are going to try to stop you from doing things. Don't stop yourself. I found out more details about the show in Scotland before I agreed to go. It was going to be called *New York Stand-up Comedy* and it would consist of me and two of my friends from the club - Larry Amoros and Bill McCarty. We would be provided with airfare, accommodations and $1,000 a week for three weeks. Sounded good to me.

The festival didn't begin until summer and since it was February and freezing in New York, I decided to go back home to Miami to visit my dad and Agatha for a week. The minute I saw my dad at the airport, I knew something was wrong. He was extremely pale and, though he was happy to see me, I sensed it was forced. On the way to the car, he told me Agatha had died. It had happened about a month before and he just couldn't tell me on the phone. She'd died in her sleep. She was 14 and it was time, but when my dad opened the garage door and she wasn't there to greet me, everything felt wrong.

As long as I could remember, we'd always had a dog. It's amazing that an animal that occupies such a small physical space can create an emptiness of such magnitude when no longer there. An aura of sadness permeated every room in the house.

Agatha's death had hit my dad hard. She was his only companion for the last five years. I noticed he had removed all the pictures of her that had been scattered around the house. Pictures of my mother, Tiny and Dagny had vanished as well. He didn't want to look at anything that died. My dad even replaced the flowers in the planter on the porch with plastic ones. I suggested maybe he get another dog and that went over badly. He was adamant.

"No more dogs. I ain't going through this again."

I didn't argue. I knew he meant it.

My father had never been a social person, but with Agatha gone, I already sensed him becoming even more isolated. He had taped cardboard over his bedroom window. He said the street light bothered him. With me there, he wouldn't answer the phone. He said I was the only one he wanted to talk to.

"If someone wants to get in touch with me they can write me a letter," he said. That wasn't as easy as it sounded. My father no longer received his mail at the house. He had rented a post office box downtown. He didn't want the mailman to know where he lived.

The night before I left to go back to New York, my father took a stack of photos out of a drawer and said, "Do you want these pictures of your mother?"

I said, "Of course, but don't you want them?"

"No. I was going to throw them away, but I won't if you want them."

My dad was not a sentimental kind of guy. A few days after my mom died, he put all her clothes in bags, took them somewhere and they were never seen again. I loved glass animals and had a collection of them on my desk in my bedroom. When I left, he threw them all away. At least he asked me if I wanted the pictures. I took all the photographs of Agatha, Tiny, my mom and one or two of Dagny as well. I felt a little guilty leaving my dad there in Miami all by himself, but I had several comedy jobs later that month and had to get back to my life. In New York, I was not only working in the clubs for cab fare, I was getting booked in comedy clubs around the country. Because of my television appearances, I was no longer the middle act; I was now the headliner.

THE NO-DOG YEARS

I love to shop after a bad relationship. I go out and buy a new outfit and it makes me feel better. In fact, sometimes, if I see a really great outfit, I'll break up with someone on purpose. Once I saw a great outfit and I wasn't dating anyone, so I went up and hugged a stranger and slapped him and bought it.

Eight

In August 1984, I was on my way to Scotland with Larry, Bill and Bill's girlfriend now wife, Patty. We were met by the producer at the airport and from there all of us caught a train to Edinburgh. The producer's name was Martin. He was extremely polite, efficient and witty. I liked him immediately and wondered about his romantic situation until I saw him light up a cigarette. Back in those days, smoking was the norm in the clubs. Very often the audience members in the front seats would be smoking and it was difficult to breathe. Most nights I arrived back at my apartment smelling like the Marlboro Man. One of my rules was that I couldn't ever get involved with someone who smoked. So that was that.

New York Stand-up Comedy was a big hit at the Edinburgh Festival. We were the first of the new-wave of American club comedians to visit Britain. I was asked to appear on a couple of national TV chat shows, interviewed by the British equivalents of Letterman and Carson. Being in a hit, sold-out show makes you feel younger, prettier and thinner. The smiles on people's faces are always broader when they are making money. Therefore, it was a magical summer. Edinburgh itself is visually stunning with its dominating medieval castle on a hill directly in the middle of the town. Flowers are ubiquitous and the houses are all perfectly lined up like freshly-straightened teeth. A Scottish Norman Rockwell painting is how I would describe that picturesque city. At least, in the summer.

Many Edinburgh residents rent out their houses for a month during the festival. The four of us lived in a three-bedroom house that featured a back yard in full bloom. Martin was an extremely conscientious producer. He, his business partner Andre and the four of us ate in wonderful restaurants and took day trips into the countryside. Martin had an Australian girlfriend who was away for the summer, just as I still had that lingering, dangling, strangling relationship back in New York.

Back home in September, I resumed my regular comedy life: clubs, writing and working. Although I was firmly a comedian, I was still taking ballet, singing and acting lessons, reasoning I needed to keep all those muscles in shape. For some reason that made sense at the time I had added swimming 100 laps a day at a health club to my schedule. The relationship I had presumed would get better was getting worse. I was unhappy and the exhaustion avoidance technique was not working for me anymore. I was crying about three times a day - not over issues that were inconsequential, but literally over nothing. I would be sitting at home and just begin to cry.

Here's another rule I try to live my life by: if something is not working, I attempt to solve the problem. Complaining about it isn't going to help. I decided it was time for therapy. My friend Julie knew a psychotherapist; I asked for her phone number and began seeing Susan the following week.

That first session was almost 40 years ago but it is still fresh in my mind. Susan asked me if I had a happy childhood. I answered, "Yes, but my mother died."

"When did she die?"

"When I was 13."

"How long was she sick?"

"About eight years."

"Tell me about it," she said.

So, I told her my story. Susan began to cry. I'm not sure if this happens to a lot of patients - that they depress their therapists - but I succeeded. Obviously, I had never dealt with the death of my mother and needed to talk to someone about it. I saw Susan twice a week for about a year.

We talked about everything. My mother, my father and my relationships were all out on the table like a psychological smorgasbord. Susan didn't offer lots of solutions. She just asked lots of questions and I provided the answers which caused me to think about why I was behaving in ways that were clearly self-destructive.

For instance, why was I always picking men who were emotionally and physically unavailable? Men who were self-involved and overly occupied with their careers? Over the years I had studiously refused to be involved with anyone in show business. Why? I realized I didn't think I was interesting enough for someone to spend a great deal of time with. I had spent so much of my time on my own when I was growing up, I felt I should only be a guest star in a relationship and not a co-star. Brad 3 was studying to be a doctor and if you want to be treated like a side effect, my advice is to date someone in medical school. To be fair to him, at the age we were then we were looking for different types of relationships. There is one thing a successful relationship and comedy have in common. Timing.

There was a man in my building who had asked me out a few times and I had always said, "No."

Susan asked, "Why?"

I said, "Because he lives in my building. I don't want to have to see someone in the elevator every day if it turns into a debacle."

"What if he's a nice person and you're discounting him because he lives in your building?"

"I'll think about it," I replied.

Enter Brad 3 ½. I'm not giving him a whole Brad. You'll have to keep reading if you want to know why.

I went out to dinner with Brad 3 ½ a few times and it turned out he was a successful business man in his thirties who had an acceptable sense of humor. He was supportive of my comedy career and we went to great restaurants in New York that I never knew existed. I met all of his friends and we spent time at his house in the country. He asked me to accompany him on a vacation to an exotic tropical island. I said "yes," and he booked the trip. Our room was a hut on a private beach. We played tennis and swam every day. The food was fantastic. I even enjoyed getting horribly sea-sick on a fishing expedition! I spent days with one person and he found me interesting. Susan had been correct. By judging a man by where he lived, I was cutting off possibilities.

When we returned from our trip, I noticed Brad 3 ½ becoming distant. He wasn't calling me every day and he hadn't made a dinner date and had not visited the club.

One evening, I answered the phone and Brad 3 ½ had some news for me.

"I have to break off this relationship," he explained. "It's getting serious and I can never marry you because you're Jewish."

"You're kidding!" I said in shock.

"No, I'm not. I'm not going to marry someone Jewish. This has to stop now."

I wish I could have thought of something witty or cutting to say, but I was dumb-founded. I just hung up and began to shiver and shake. What just happened?

You think I was upset? You should have seen Susan!

"Well, let's think of all the wonderful experiences you've had that you wouldn't have had if you had never gone out with him," she rationalized.

"That's well and good, but now the rat is in my building and I'm going to have to see him in the damn elevator."

"He's the one who is going to feel like a jerk," she responded.

Skipping ahead, the next time I saw Brad 3 ½ was over 20 years later in my VIP Meet and Greet line in Las Vegas. He paid extra to get to meet me in person. He wanted to know if I was still married. I said, "Yes. Very." He gave me his card in case I ever wanted to call him. Surprisingly, I never did.

I still continued to see Susan, even though, thanks to her, I no longer felt comfortable waiting for the elevator door to open and every so often thought about walking down 30 flights of stairs instead. One session I had with Susan was totally transforming. I had a dream that I was sitting behind the wheel of a car, unable to drive it because there were strings attached to my arms. My father was standing on the hood of the car pulling the strings. I told my dream to Susan. She said, "I don't think I have to explain that dream to you. I think we know what is happening here." As independent as I was, in certain ways, I was still being controlled by my past. I decided after that session that I was going to learn how to drive. I used my "if other people can do it so can I" argument and the following week, I was behind a wheel driving very slowly up Riverside Drive with my instructor, Ralph.

I was still performing at Catch and one night, after my set, Rodney Dangerfield came up to me. "Rita," he said, "You're very funny. It's a tough business. Sometimes you never make it."

"Thank you, I think," I replied.

Rodney was a character. I'd met him a few times in the bar at Catch and actually sold him a "So fat" joke. Here it is. "She was so fat, I got on top of her and my ears popped." Not exactly Nobel Prize material but it earned me 50 bucks. I liked Rodney and always thought he was a terrific comedian.

He asked me if I would like to be on *The Rodney Dangerfield Young Comedians' Special* on HBO. Would I?! The line-up was Sam Kinison, Louie Anderson, Bob Saget, Richie Gold, Bob Nelson and me. We taped it in Rodney's club on First Avenue. I had no idea it would have the impact it did. People still come up to me and remind me of some of the jokes I told on that show.

We all did really well, but it was Sam's night. I remember his look of triumph as he left the stage. He knew he had just performed five minutes that would change his life. Looking at it 30 years later, his material would today be excoriated for its misogyny, homophobia and political incorrectness. At that time, though, its originality and outrageousness made it breathtaking. I always forgave any taste-lapse because the material so clearly came from a place of pain and truth. And Sam's delivery, birthed from his Pentecostal preaching background, was unique. His primal scream of marital pain never failed to make me laugh.

That special aired in August 1985 and the Kinison and Rudner paths occasionally crossed after that. I remember a fun night in West Palm Beach. Sam was performing a huge concert in the area and I was playing a sell-out run at a local club. Sam dropped by to watch my second show (and probably try to score some drugs, let's be honest) and I convinced him to come on stage and perform a little. We spent an hour or so chatting and laughing together before he was swept up again in the whirlwind of mayhem that was his life.

Seven years later, in 1992, I wrote a screenplay for Sam and I to consider doing together. Sam would play a man who was on death row, got pardoned and returned home to find me now renting his apartment. I was "Hollywood-hot" at that moment and all the studios were interested in what I came up with. Unfortunately, Sam was "Hollywood-cold"; he was considered too unreliable, having recently quit a film mid-production. He liked our script and wanted to do it. He was living out in Malibu, and he and his girlfriend Malika were planning to marry. He was confident Hollywood would eventually forgive him and then maybe we could make that movie together?

Five days after Sam and Malika were married, Sam was killed by a drunk teenager in a car crash as he drove to Laughlin to perform a show. I was booked to perform in the same theater a week later and I will never forget driving past the place where my friend had died a week earlier. He was 38, three months younger than me.

But let's back up those seven years, returning to 1985, the year of the Rodney HBO special. Another television gig popped up around the same time. *CBS This Morning* had decided to use

RITA RUDNER

comedians. I became a regular. I arrived at the studio at 6:30 in the morning and went into make-up. I was on camera at around 7:30. I would be done at 8:00. It's never easy to make people laugh before 8:00 in the morning. I remember once following a segment on teenage suicide. Nevertheless, it was a great gig and it lasted until the research came out and showed that no one wanted to laugh before 8:00 in the morning.

By this time, I had a manager and an agent and everyone was pushing me towards TV. Like lots of women my age, my television idol growing up was Mary Tyler Moore. In fact, one of the comedians at Catch – Gilbert Gottfried – nicknamed me Jewish Tyler Moore.

After videotaping an audition in New York for a situation comedy that was to be shot in Hollywood, I was told ABC executives wanted to see me in person in Los Angeles. I couldn't believe this opportunity was actually happening. I was flown first class to California and picked up by a driver who deposited me in an overly-marbled hotel in Century City. When I gave my name to the person at the front desk, he handed me the keys to my room and told me, "Everything has been taken care of." My room overlooked a street called Avenue of the Stars. How Hollywood was that? I called my friend Marjorie in Manhattan to tell her because I knew she'd get a kick out of it.

"Is there a smaller street next to it called 'Avenue of the Co-Stars'?" she asked.

I told you Marjorie was funny.

I found a manila envelope in my room containing the pages of the script that I was to use at my audition. It also contained instructions about where to be and when. At two o'clock I walked across the street and read the script to three executives seated in a barren room. There was next to no reaction. I left. I went back to my hotel room and sat by the phone. Nothing. Finally, at 5:00 p.m., I called the casting director.

84

"I didn't hear anything. What should I do?" I asked.

"Well, you didn't get the job. I guess you should go back to New York, unless you have people you want to visit here. You have your plane ticket and the room for the night."

"Is a car picking me up?"

"No, call a cab and send us the receipt. We'll reimburse you."

I couldn't wait to get back to New York. I called the airline and flew back that night in a rejection coma. This is why life-long friends are so important. If your self-worth is dependent upon the fickle nature of show business, it's only a matter of time before you become emotionally bankrupt.

I met my latest boyfriend in Australia because I couldn't find a man in this hemisphere. There's a shortage. You know, they came out with that study in Newsweek last year. It said that if you're a single woman over 30, there's a less than 20% chance you'll ever get married. They should do another survey. They should find out how many women over 30 ever bought Newsweek again.

Nine

Back in New York, I was still seeing Susan, booking clubs and had appeared a few more times on *Late Night with David Letterman*. One day I received a phone call from Martin, the producer of the Edinburgh Festival show.

"I'm putting another stand-up show together and I'd love you to be in it. Do you want to come to Australia?"

"Australia. That's kind of far away."

"Yes. You would have to take a plane. My treat," he dead-panned.

The job sounded appealing, but at this point I was still reeling from my trip to Los Angeles. I said, "No, but maybe another time." Martin took three other comedians to Australia and it was a big success. He kept in touch and wrote letters to me from time to time. You remember letters? Those pieces of paper that used to arrive in the mail that weren't bills. He also arrived in New York one weekend and took me with him to see a few Broadway shows whose overseas' rights he was interested in. Before he left, he arranged US Open tickets for Larry Amoros and me, courtesy of Ivan Lendl, at that time the number one male tennis player in the world. No romantic involvement happened with the interesting, twenty-something Englishman; he was still with his Australian girlfriend and still smoking.

Meanwhile, more and more comedians were moving west. We all wanted to be on television and the majority of television shows were made in Hollywood; in particular, *The Tonight Show*. While David Letterman was more a comedic contemporary, Johnny Carson was a legend. To be called over to sit on the couch after your comedy set was the ultimate late-night honor. I watched my (male) friends move, one by one, to Los Angeles, perform on *The Tonight Show* and get TV situation comedy deals. Although the thought of moving coasts made me a little queasy, I had my driver's license and a singer friend who had moved to Los Angeles had a guest house for rent. I rented my apartment to another comedian for six months and decided to give it a real try. If other people can do it....... I think you know the rest.

You're probably going to think this sounds stupid because I was 31. Getting off a plane, renting a car and driving on a freeway would not have been a big deal to a normal person. It was to me. No GPS systems then, just me in a car that resembled a tuna fish can on wheels and an unruly map. I'm surprised I wasn't arrested that day for driving too slowly on the 405. My singer friend, Vicki, had become a successful writer in Hollywood and had married a fellow-writer. They lived in a vast house up a hill so steep that a goat would take a cab. Turning from the narrow, winding road into their garage took me a good 20 minutes, and I'm sure that garage still bears a few scars from my multiple attempts at entry. If there is ever a contest where I have to park a car in a garage, I would be foolish to enter. On the bright side, the guest house was perfect. I may not have been on television like my idol Mary Tyler Moore, but my little one room apartment was almost identical to the one she lived in on her eponymous TV show. This was not an omen.

The Improv on Melrose Avenue was my first port of call. Most of my Catch people were performing there. Budd Friedman was the owner of the club and the emcee most nights. Budd truly loves comedy. He was kind to comedians and I've never heard a bad word spoken about him. His wife, Alex was also at the club most nights and the two of them provided a friendly, nurturing atmosphere. One of my first jobs in Los Angeles was on Budd's *An Evening at the Improv* TV show.

I had heard about the Comedy Store on Sunset Boulevard for years. It was famous for introducing stars like Robin Williams,

Richard Pryor, Michael Keaton, David Letterman and so many more. I performed there a few times but I never really felt I belonged. Also, it was almost impossible for me to back out of the Comedy Store parking lot. Most nights another comedian would come out and back my car out for me. I can do lots of things well; backing up in a car isn't one of them.

Jim McCawley was the comedy booker for *The Tonight Show*. He was going to be at the Improv to look at new comics one week and Budd put me on the list. When the evening came, I had my set ready. There were three or four comics auditioning for Jim that night. When it was my turn, Jim listened for a minute or two, got up and walked out of the room. He talked to me for a few minutes before he left that night. He said I wasn't funny, had bad timing and Johnny wouldn't like me. So much for my master plan to appear on *The Tonight Show*.

I had a problem with Jim's opinion. If I wasn't funny, why were people laughing? Why was I getting booked all over the country and appearing on other television shows? Aside from that setback, I was actually enjoying my time in Los Angeles. At the Improv one evening, I called home for messages. Martin was in town and staying at the Beverly Wilshire hotel on his way back to Australia. After my set, I decided to stop by. I called from the lobby.

"Hi Martin, it's Rita. I'm downstairs."

"Oh, Rita. Hi," he slurred.

"Are you sleeping?"

"No," he lied. "Come on up."

I came up and he opened an over-priced bottle of champagne from his mini-bar. Still only in his twenties, the list of productions he had already been involved with was impressive and diverse – from The Royal Shakespeare Company to James Brown. His biggest and ongoing success was the arena world tour of Olympic ice-skating champions, Jayne Torvill and Christopher Dean. They won gold medals with perfect marks, dancing to Ravel's *Boléro*. Having started as a comedy writer and performer, Martin's penchant for comedy still remained.

"Have you changed your mind about coming to Australia?" he asked. "There's a brand-new theater opening on the Gold Coast and I'm putting together another stand-up show to christen it."

I'd heard from my friends who had done the first Australian tour about how much fun they'd had. This time I said, "Yes, count me in."

My father wasn't happy about it. "Jesus Christ, Rita Carol, first you go to Los Angeles, now you're going to Australia. Where are you going to go next? The moon?"

That December, Larry Amoros, Richard Jeni and I were on our way to Australia. Not quite the moon, but close. Our destination was the Gold Coast, which is the Miami Beach of Australia. There were no direct flights, so we had a stopover in Sydney. Ever the thoughtful producer, Martin had an associate, Diana, meet us in Sydney while we waited for our next plane. Diana lit up a cigarette and said, "I'm so angry at Martin. He stopped smoking. I've been trying to quit for years and he just did it so easily."

My eyebrows raised, "He stopped smoking?"

"Yes, I'm furious. It's been six months since he's had a cigarette."

Hmmm.

Martin met us at the Gold Coast airport and drove us to an absolutely beautiful hotel. Then he drove us to the hotel where we were staying. Okay, that's a joke; we were actually staying at the beautiful hotel. My next goal was to find out what happened to Myrtle (not the girlfriend's real name.) Over dinner that evening I subtly asked, "How's Myrtle?"

"Myrtle decided to stay in London. She didn't want to come with me to Australia and we'd been having trouble anyway so that's the end of that. How's Brad?" (Not my old boyfriend's real name.)

"He's dead to me," I replied, understating the situation.

Martin and I had always liked each other. I really wasn't thinking long term with this one, but Susan encouraged me to throw away my list of requirements of the type of man I should be with. Martin was in show business. He was three years and nine months younger than I was and he didn't live in America. However, I'd known him for years, he was good looking, funny, trustworthy, considerate and had recently become available. It was December, which is summer in Australia, and I figured it was time to have some fun. I'm not that great at flirting, but I remember that wherever he sat, I sat next to him. I made him laugh. He made me laugh. He got the idea.

He said, "You know, I'm going to have to break my rule of never getting involved with people I'm working with."

I said, "I agree with you. I think that's what you're going to have to do."

We waited until the show opened to close the deal. The next morning Martin had to leave early to take care of some business. Past thoughts coursed through my mind. Was this a good idea? What if we don't get along? What if I'm going to have to see him every day? Is this another elevator situation?

My fears were assuaged, (how's that for a word?) when he called at 11:00 that morning and said he'd booked us a table for lunch.

He drove me to Oscar's, a seafood restaurant directly on the beach. We ordered the seafood platter, a wonderful array of scallops, lobster, shrimp and a few *what the hell are those and are they moving*? Everything was wonderful between us. We were in that blissful beginning of a relationship stage, but there was one thing going horribly wrong. The show was a flop. Not because we weren't funny, but because Martin had not been told that the community had voted against building a theater. They had voted for their tax money to be used for a dam instead. The local council had ignored the citizens' wishes, so now there was an active boycott by the locals and the taxi drivers were refusing to bring tourists over the bridge. Once you've eliminated locals and tourists in your audience, you're pretty much left with wildlife. Martin did everything he could to convince people to attend. He persuaded the local paper to send a reviewer. A good review would certainly be an incentive. The reviewer hated the show. He found fault with every comedian. I had a joke about worms being both male and female. The punchline was something like, "I guess God made one worm, looked at it and thought 'This thing is never going to get a date.'" The reviewer made mention of me making a disgusting joke about copulating worms. There is an old show business saying, "If the audience doesn't want to come, you can't stop 'em." They really didn't want to come.

It's one thing to be pleasant and charming when the show you are producing is a hit. It is another thing to be pleasant and charming when the show you are producing is going down the toilet. Martin asked me if I would move in with him to save some money on my hotel room. I packed my bags. Martin and his Australian partner were living in a four-bedroom penthouse overlooking the Pacific Ocean. It wasn't really a hardship. I had been in the penthouse for less than a week when Martin received a phone call. It was from England and it was Myrtle. She had changed her mind. She felt she made a terrible mistake and wanted to come live with Martin in Australia.

Alarm bells went off in my head. I immediately thought of Brad 3 and his "I really like you but I still have to see other people" routine.

I heard only Martin's end of the conversation. He said, "I'm involved with someone else now. No, I don't think you should come. If you do, I can have lunch with you, but that's it. Sorry. Bye."

I was shocked. I'd only been involved with men who couldn't make up their minds.

"So, was that Myrtle?" I asked.

"Yes. I told you it was over and it's over. "

We looked at each other and did what not many people who are newly in love do. I said, "I've been thinking. Let's rent a typewriter."

He said, "I've been thinking the same thing. Let's write a movie script."

As mentioned previously, Martin had written comedy in London for the BBC. Prior to that, he wrote and performed sketches for a comedy troupe at Cambridge University. I had written jokes and sketches with my friend Marjorie, but we both always wanted to try writing a movie.

Martin and I sat in a penthouse overlooking the ocean and attempted to write our first movie script. The show continued to lose money. I felt somewhat guilty. If I had said, "No, I won't come to Australia," maybe none of this would have happened. But then we wouldn't have gotten together, so there you go. The negative into positive situation applies once again.

We celebrated Christmas in the Australian penthouse. The guests included, Doris and Lois (the publicity team working on the show), Martin's partner Michael and his girlfriend Jackie, Michael's three children from his first marriage, Larry, Richard, me, Michael's mother Edna, a co-worker who had just been jilted and a few more people from here and there. Everybody participated in the cooking, the eating and the cleaning up. Because I had next to no family, this collective, chaotic experience was exhilarating.

The show however, continued to fail. One evening, we arrived at the theater and the parking lot was full.

Martin said with relief, "It's finally working. People have realized it's a fun evening!"

A few minutes later, people exited the theater and got into their cars. We found out that there had been a local art show earlier in the evening that was well-attended by friends and relatives.

At the end of the financial debacle, Richard and Larry flew back to Los Angeles. I accompanied Martin back to his apartment in

Melbourne. He lived in a lovely part of Melbourne called Toorak. Every morning we walked to the local coffee bar and order cappuccinos and read the paper. I stayed for a few weeks and then we both had to get back to reality. Martin was continuing his arena show starring ice skating duo Torvill and Dean. (That show was thankfully making money!) And I had bookings in a variety of comedy clubs across the USA. He promised to visit me soon.

I just bought my own house. You know what it had to say on the deed? "Rita Rudner. A single woman." It looked so lonely. I said, "Can't you at least put that I have lots of friends?"

Ten

A few months later, I readied my one room apartment in Los Angeles for Martin's scheduled arrival from Australia. At the same time, I had just been booked to appear on my third HBO special called *Women of the Night*. The special would feature Paula Poundstone, Judy Tenuta, Ellen DeGeneres and me. It was to be hosted by one of the funniest men ever, Martin Short.

My Martin was underwhelmed by my living arrangements. He stood in the middle of the room and said, "Where's the rest of it?"

"This is it."

"Where do we sleep?"

"I pull out the sofa bed."

"You've been saving money since you were 16. Why don't you buy a house?"

It never occurred to me to buy a house. I was 32 and had just bought my first car: a used Volvo with an interior the color of poodle poo. My comedian friends told me that I looked like I was driving a hat. It was my very own hat/car and I loved it. It went anywhere I wanted it to go.

In preparation for the TV special, Martin and I spent every evening at the Improv. He had toured many of the comedians at the club around either Scotland or Australia, so he fit right in to the comedy vibe. Some of my friends who were staying at the Magic Hotel gave him a "Welcome to Los Angeles" party which was so thoughtful. Almost all people I had spent years with at Catch were now living in Los Angeles. It made a city that can be extremely unfriendly a lot more comfortable.

The stress level of filming a special is always high, but it is especially intense when there are four performers. You really don't want to be the one that bombs. Luckily, all of us did well that evening. *Women of the Night* turned out to be a well-received special for HBO and we all saw our popularity rise. The four of us are acquaintances, but never became close friends. In fact, I don't have any close female comedian friends. I think this is because two female comedians were never hired to work together. Whenever I was hired for a gig on the road, it was always either me and a male or me and two males. Hopefully, it's different now, but female comedians in my generation didn't really bond and that's regretful.

A factor that always affects me when I'm filming something for television, is how far away the audience is compared to how close they are in a club or theater. That's why you see many comedian hosts in late night shows build a lip from the stage so they can be closer to the audience. The only thing I insist upon when I do a private show for a company is that the people be close to the stage. If there is a dance floor between the comedian and the attendees, the connection between the performer and the audience is non-existent. Here's another tip: comedy never works outside. I don't know why, but for jokes to be effective, you need a ceiling. Preferably a low ceiling. And also, people should be seated close together. The old adage that "laughter is contagious" is true. So, for all wannabe comedians out there, avoid playing parks and planetariums. Also, try to avoid opening for rock bands. People who see rock bands aren't in the mood to listen to carefully crafted jokes. I opened for a rock band once early in my career. I can't remember the name of the band, but I do remember the person in the front row throwing up.

Martin eventually flew back to Australia to co-produce both *The Moscow Circus* and the next installment of *The Torvill & Dean World Tour* and I followed a few months later so we could spend the Christmas vacation together before I had to head back home for shows my agent had booked. This was the very definition of a long-distance relationship, one of us always having to fly 8,000 miles to see the other one. I was still waiting for the whole thing to blow up.

How was this ever going to work? I was in love with a man who lived in Australia! Maybe Susan had given me another bum steer.

That December, Martin greeted me at Sydney airport with flowers. He rented a swanky apartment in the center of the city for us to stay in during the run of the circus. He proposed to me on that trip by first giving me a ring from Walgreens. I was suspicious when I looked at it closely and realized that it was adjustable. He then followed it up with a real engagement ring. I said, "Yes." I was definitely marrying a man with a sense of humor. Living arrangements were not going to be a problem, he assured me. He would move to California. What about his apartments in Melbourne and London? He would rent them or sell them. Wow! This man must really love me. What about his business? He had figured that out too.

It turned out he had grown tired of commuting between Australia and London, and Los Angeles seemed a good compromise. Always slightly ahead of the game, he already had a portable Toshiba computer and could get on something he called the internet by somehow attaching a phone receiver to his computer. A rock band's tour manager in Australia had introduced him to it. "It's just a rock'n'roll thing now," Martin told me. "However, soon it's going to take over the world and become how people communicate. I can run my business from anywhere."

When I returned to Los Angeles I decided it was time to search for a house. Martin rightly pointed out that we wouldn't be happy living in a room where, when we laid down on our bed, our feet were in the kitchen. I bought a house off of Laurel Canyon that looked like it was straight out of Hansel and Gretel. The beams in the ceiling were railroad ties and the windows in the living room were made of stained glass. It was 900 square feet and the washing machine was in the backyard. The bedroom was so tiny it could only house a full mattress and the bureau was situated in the hall. The garage only had enough room for half a car.

"What is it with you and small spaces?" Martin asked.

I had been living in a New York City apartment for all of my adult life. To me it was roomy. Martin moved to Los Angeles, continuing to work with his partners back in Australia. He was also part owner of a comedy club in Melbourne and was booking American comedians to perform in this venue. I enrolled in a screenwriting course and continued to work around the country as well as perform at the Improv when I was in town. I was also still attending ballet class whenever I could.

One day Martin asked, "Why are you still going to ballet class? You haven't been a dancer for years."

"I don't know," I replied. "That's just what I do."

"Well, don't. Let's go out to lunch. Let's go to the movies. Let's try and write something. I've moved out here from Australia and you're going to ballet class. You're a comedian now. I think that dancey part of your life is over."

He had a point. I know this isn't a unique conclusion to arrive at, but compromise is key in relationships. I could no longer do exactly what I wanted to do all the time. It was time to break some of my overly disciplined habits and learn to relax some of my Rita Rules.

I was headlining comedy shows all over the country but *The Tonight Show* still eluded me. Every time I walked on stage, Jim McCawley, the show's comedy booker, automatically walked out. One night he was sitting with Budd Friedman and Budd's wife, Alex. As I walked on stage, Jim got up and started to leave.

Alex relayed her conversation with him to me later. She said, "What's wrong with you? Rita is very funny. Sit down and listen to her." Jim sat. I had a good set.

He met me out at the bar and said, "I think you're almost ready to be on *The Tonight Show*. You just have to work on your timing. I think you should watch Mary Lou Retton."

"Mary Lou Retton?" I replied.

"Yes, she has very good timing."

I didn't really understand what he was talking about, but I didn't think I should bring up the fact that Mary Lou was a gymnast. I just agreed that Mary Lou Retton had very good timing. He then said, "You have to reverse the beginning of your act and put it at the end. I'll come see you at the Comedy and Magic Club tomorrow night."

The Comedy and Magic Club was a venue in Hermosa Beach where many comedians went to try out material away from the center of Los Angeles. I said, "See you there."

The next night at the Comedy and Magic Club, I reversed my act the way Jim had suggested. The set wasn't nearly as effective. To his credit, Jim said "Go back to the way you were doing it before. I'll call your agent tomorrow and book you on the show."

So, if it hadn't been for Alex Friedman, I would have probably never appeared on *The Tonight Show*, and if it hadn't been for Mary Lou Retton, it would have made no difference.

Driving onto the NBC lot was exciting, especially because Martin and I got lost a few times on the way. Luckily, we knew we were directionally-challenged and began our journey early. I quickly found my favorite place, the make-up room, and reviewed my set silently. Returning to my dressing room, I waited until I was called. I kept waiting. The show was over and they had run out of time. Jim apologized and said he would re-book me soon. I wonder if they would have run out of time if I had been Mary Lou Retton.

Believe it or not, I was bumped again the next time I was scheduled to be on the show. I finally appeared for the first time on what was called "The Bump Show" in the spring of 1988. It consisted of me, Ritch Shydner and Darryl Sivad. We had all been bumped a few times and it was Johnny's idea to have a show just featuring us. We were all called over to the couch to talk to Johnny after our sets. I couldn't believe I was sitting next to Johnny Carson. I looked at him and said, "You're Johnny Carson." He laughed and said, "And you're Rita Rudner." After years of being rejected for the show, I became a regular and Johnny Carson couldn't have been more supportive.

Shortly after my appearance on *The Tonight Show*, I was offered my first comedy job in Las Vegas. I had been to Vegas once before when I was 18, singing and dancing in an industrial show for Lincoln Continental. I still remember part of one song. Here goes: "The Continental, the Comet and the new Marquis, the mid-sized Montego and the sexy Capri, and then there's the Cougar and the great Mark 3. More kinds of cars for more kinds of people." I'll sing the tune for you if we ever meet in person. Anyway, Budd Friedman had just opened an Improv inside the Riviera Hotel and asked me to headline. Martin and I made our first of what would turn out to be many trips to Las Vegas.

Martin was fascinated with the shiny city. While I was telling jokes, he was busy exploring all the other casinos and entertainment on the Strip. He noticed that while the majority of tourists were in their thirties and forties, the performers on the strip were in their sixties and seventies. He made a mental note that Vegas might be a place ripe for younger performers. That turned out to be a lucrative thought.

There was something both glamorous and grubby about Las Vegas in the late 1980s. The lights at night were enticing but if you looked too closely you saw the wires and the dirt in between them. While I was performing at the Improv, Martin was off exploring. He had spotted an advertisement for Frank Sinatra appearing at the Golden Nugget. He bought a ticket and when he told me what he had seen that evening, I was jealous. To fulfill his contract, Frank was playing a small room while the main room was being renovated. Martin was able to experience an intimate evening with one of the great performers of all time.

After my gig in Las Vegas, Martin returned to Australia to produce a tour of the Harlem Globetrotters in Australia and New Zealand. He also decided to try another comedy show, this one in

Sydney, arguably Australia's hippest city. Me, Larry Amoros and Kelly Rogers were the three comedians. Fortunately, this show was a hit. In fact, it was so successful, we were extended. I felt I had almost made up for my disastrous first appearance on the Gold Coast.

My husband and I get along really well. We don't argue. We have a system of marital points. Whenever one of us is wrong about something, the other one gets a marital point, and at the end of the year, the loser has to take my grandmother underwear shopping.

Eleven

We returned to my Hansel and Gretel house in Laurel Canyon and one night, sitting in our living room watching television, Martin jumped up, grabbed his passport and said, "My visa is running out. We're going to have to get married." It was one of those romantic moments about which every girl dreams. The next day, Martin, dressed in his finest suit, and I, in my finest blue slacks and blue and white top, drove downtown to City Hall to begin the marital process. We couldn't find a parking space so we drove back to our cottage in the woods, still unmarried. We decided to make the event slightly more formal. We worked backwards. Where did we want to spend our honeymoon? There was a new Ritz Carlton in Laguna Beach which seemed inviting. Martin located a court house in Orange County on the way to our hotel. The following week, we again attempted marriage. This time Martin handed me a map and said, "Let's see if you can find the courthouse." Needless to say, I couldn't and we stopped at multiple gas stations to ask for directions. We arrived at the court house, wandered up to the marrying floor and stood in the marriage line.

Martin had one request of me. He said, "Please don't cry. I'm English. I'll get embarrassed."

I said, "Why would I cry? That's just silly."

It was our turn to be married. A demure lady wearing a pin that said "Phyllis" proceeded with her speech.

"Hello, my name is Phyllis and I will be marrying you today. We have two services available to you. A religious service or a civil service, which one would you prefer?"

I started laughing. The whole scene of standing in a line and getting married by Phyllis at a counter seemed hysterically funny to me. I couldn't hold it back. I couldn't stop. I saw Martin growing uncomfortable. "Phyllis, what floor are the divorces on?" he joked.

Phyllis said, "Do you want me to stop?"

I said, "No, I'll control myself."

She began the ceremony, "Do you take this man to be your lawfully wedded husband, till death do you part?"

Again, I began laughing uncontrollably. I said, "I'm so sorry" and "Yes" and then I began to cry. Not just light, civil crying, but moose-noise crying. The enormity of the event came out in primitive, heaving sounds. I hadn't thought about wearing waterproof mascara and black streaks were now cascading down my cheeks. I somehow made it through the ceremony and at the end of the undignified fiasco, we were married. June 24th, 1988.

Now this next part wasn't my fault. We had two paper cameras. One was brand new and one had only a single photo left in it. Martin grabbed the wrong camera before we left the house, so we only had one shot at a wedding picture. We went down stairs to the newspaper/candy and gum/soda stand and asked the lady behind the register to take our photo. As she did, a woman crossed behind us drinking a Diet Coke. That is our wedding picture and today it sits proudly on a shelf in my bathroom. When I was growing up, I always pictured the dream wedding: the white dress, the flowers, etc. I look back at our courthouse non-event and cherish it. I wouldn't have had it any other way.

Martin and I proceeded to try to find the new hotel. The hotel was very expensive, so we had booked a room overlooking the pool rather than overlooking the ocean. The manager found out from our friends sending us a wedding cake and congratulatory balloons that it was our honeymoon and upgraded us to a suite overlooking the Pacific. We had a fantastic three-day honeymoon. Then, back to work. I was starting an NBC television show in Los Angeles called *Funny People*, devised by George Schlatter, the producer who created *Laugh In*. Martin was due back in Australia. As I write this chapter, we have been married for almost 35 years and I'm not sure Martin has yet forgiven me for my wedding behavior.

Funny People, my first and it turned out only crack at primetime network TV, was an almost hit. The premise was a novel one: regular people sent in funny videos of themselves doing crazy things and the hosts were sent out to film segments in uncomfortable situations. A short time after *Funny People* was canceled, a show came along called *America's Funniest Home Videos*. This was an enormous hit. I wasn't in that one.

I had, however, received an offer from HBO to do my own half hour special called *One Night Stand*. It was to be filmed in San Francisco. The Fillmore was the chosen venue; a cross between a club and a theater. It was a perfect atmosphere for comedy. If you get a chance to watch it, a young David Spade plays the stage manager in the opening sketch.

My career was clicking, undoubtedly aided and abetted by Martin's advice and involvement. He tried to stay out of my professional life. It was difficult for him because he was a producer and writer and he had both feet firmly planted in show business. He had been aghast during our week in Las Vegas at how many shows I had performed for such a small fee. He also hadn't been thrilled by my manager who phoned me regularly to ask, "What's going on?"

"You see, Rita, it's the wrong way around," Martin explained. "You're supposed to phone the manager and ask him, 'What's going on?'"

My booking agent called me a lot, but mainly to ask what else I thought he might be able to do for a living because he really hated being an agent. He told me he was considering making furniture instead.

Martin worked with all the major agencies in Los Angeles when booking acts to tour Australia. He really liked the agent through whom he had booked the Harlem Globetrotters and who was coincidentally interested in comedy. Martin introduced me to this agent who did want to be an agent and he is my agent to this day: Steve Levine of ICM. Today he's a partner and the co-head of the company's Worldwide Concerts division. I hope my former agent is still happy making furniture.

Martin changed the structure of my deals at clubs and theaters. Instead of receiving a flat fee, I was now doing door deals, being paid according to how many people showed up to see me. Suddenly, my earnings escalated considerably as my popularity grew.

And as my popularity grew, the number of events we were invited to in Los Angeles increased as well. One particular movie premiere has stuck in my memory. I can't remember the film, but it must have been a big deal as it needed the use of two movie theaters in Westwood. As we approached the theatre, an elegantly dressed and coiffured older lady in a wheelchair approached me. I was getting more used to this; members of the public wanting to say hello because they felt they knew me from seeing me on television.

"Rita! I watched you on Carson. You're terrific!"

"Thank you so much. What's your name?"

The woman looked puzzled.

"I'm Ginger," she said. "Ginger Rogers."

Oh my God!

"I'm so sorry," I vamped. "I haven't got my glasses on. What a thrill to meet you. I love you."

I still can't believe Ginger Rogers liked me, although maybe she liked me a little less after I failed to recognize her. (In my defense, it's not like she was wearing tap shoes or anything.) I thought of my mother – the wannabe dancer who had no doubt lined up to see Astaire & Rogers movies back in the day – could she ever have imagined that one day I'd be complimented by Ginger Rogers? ("No" is the easy answer to that one).

Talking of parents, I thought it might be time for Martin to meet my father. You'll notice I waited until after we were married to introduce the two of them. I'm not stupid. I had already met Martin's parents and that had gone reasonably well so, two down, one to go. I hadn't seen my dad for a while and living alone had caused him to become even more eccentric. The inside of the house was covered in a thick layer of dust. He had fired his cleaning person years ago and decided he would vacuum a part of a rug every six months. All the windows were covered with cardboard because he didn't want anyone to know whether he was home or not. My room had become a dark, moldy cave. As Martin and I sat on my bed, we noticed that the sheets were crunchy.

I asked my father, "Dad, are these sheets clean?"

He replied, "Yes, no one has slept on them since you left."

"They've been on my bed for three years?"

"I guess so."

Later that evening, I saw my dad peeking through the cardboard taped to his window.

"Dad, what are you looking at?"

"It's the woman who lives in the house across the street. There's very strange activity."

"What's going on?" I asked.

"A car pulls up and someone goes inside. They stay for a while and then they leave. What does that say to you?"

"She has friends?" I answered.

"She's a prostitute," he declared.

My father definitely had too much time on his hands. According to him, there was another house where people were operating a drug cartel and another couple on the block were swingers. In reality, there was only one person on the block who was behaving badly and it was my father. One of my theories is that people always need someone around that they trust to tell them when they're acting crazily. You don't have to live alone to be alone. The very rich and famous suffer from the same syndrome, because the people surrounding them are being paid and are therefore afraid to tell the person who is paying them they're crazy. Someone should have told

Elvis to put down the gun. You turn off a television, you don't shoot it. Someone should have mentioned to Michael Jackson that he was an adult and it was time to get off the Ferris wheel and put down the monkey. One of Prince's friends should have mentioned that he should eat something. Those extraordinary people might have graced us with their talents a little longer had they been so advised.

The next day, Martin and I decided to walk around Coconut Grove. When I was growing up, the Grove had kind of a hippie vibe, but the area had been transformed into an upscale shopping mall. My father hadn't kept up with the changes and warned me not to take my handbag because people would kill me. I said Martin would protect me if someone tried to mug me in Saks.

My dad dropped us off and said, "Call me and I'll come pick you up. You don't want to walk home. They'll kill you."

Martin and I wandered around the shops for a while and ate a leisurely lunch. When it was time to go back to my dirty house, we didn't want to bother my father, so we walked back home. I rang the doorbell and no one answered. I rang it again. Nothing. I began yelling "Dad, dad" outside. Panic set in.

"Martin, what if he's dead?"

"He can't be dead. We saw him three hours ago and he wasn't even sick," Martin replied logically.

"Well, why won't he answer the door?"

"That I don't know."

I rang the doorbell and yelled for a few more minutes, but there was still zero response. I decided to call him from our neighbor's house. Clara was our last original neighbor and I had known her since I was six, so she wasn't on my dad's list of criminals. Luckily, Clara was home. I called my dad. He answered the phone.

"Dad, are you okay?" I asked.

"Yes," he replied. "But I can't come pick you up right now. There's a crazy person outside who keeps ringing my doorbell and screaming, 'Dad.'"

"That'll be me."

"Oh. I told you I would pick you up. What are you doing here?"

"We walked back. Just open the door."

"You walked back? With your handbag? I told you, they'll kill you."

I think you can understand why I didn't introduce my father to Martin until after we were married.

We just bought a new house together. We love our house, but we made some terrible mistakes. We hired the Vegetarian Moving Company. They were too weak to lift anything.

I had to deal with workmen because of course the house wasn't finished. When you move in, it never is. You know, some of these workmen have real attitudes. I didn't know this. The painter came in. I said, "We have some holes over here. Could you fill these in, please?" You know what he said? "Lady, I don't spackle. I don't sand and I don't tape. I just paint." Then the exterminator came in. I said, "Kill the painter."

Twelve

In 1989, HBO offered me my own situation comedy pilot and agreed to my writing it with Martin. Chris Albrecht, whom I originally met at the Improv in NYC, was now the Head of Original Programming at HBO. Sometimes, compromise makes for a great product. It depends on the people involved envisioning the same tone of program. I had a built-in problem. I was popular on HBO, which was a pay cable channel. The two elements that separated pay cable from network television were swearing and nudity. I didn't swear and I like to wear clothes. I was not a natural fit. We also had separate factions of HBO telling us what they thought should definitely be included in the pilot. The head of HBO in the early 90s, Michael Fuchs, was heavily into politics so there had to be a political element in the script. We ended up with me working for a mayor. Chris wanted the first scene to be me in bed with my boyfriend. I suggested we combine the two plots and have me in bed with my boyfriend and a mayor. Martin and I tried to twist and turn the best we could between what we thought would be picked up for a series and what I was comfortable with. HBO also insisted the pilot be filmed in a studio with no live audience. My background was theatre and comedy clubs. I was used to performing in front of people. Needless to say, the pilot of *RITA* never saw the light of day and that was probably a good thing. *Dream On* was the show they picked up that year and it was a much better fit for HBO. Chris offered me my own one-hour special as a consolation prize.

I had gone from five minutes on that first Catch special, to ten with Rodney, to 15 with *Women of the Night*, to the *One Night Stand* half hour and this was to be my first one hour special. I really stepped on every rung of the special ladder. *Born to be Mild* was to be filmed in Cleveland at the Palace Theatre. This was the beginning of the gown idea. I have very little fashion sense. In fact, when I was traveling extensively and spending time in airports, I dressed so plainly that people repeatedly asked me if I was a flight attendant. Martin, on the other hand, has quite a bit of fashion sense and, being a producer, he had a vision of what image I should portray on stage. We went shopping for my first gown and found it in a boutique on Third Avenue.

Born to be Mild turned out to be an extremely popular special and I began to get offers to open for big acts in Las Vegas. I opened for the Everly Brothers, Frankie Valli and the Four Seasons, Tony Bennett and Julio Iglesias. Opening for famous people can be slightly treacherous. I remember the mostly female audience at Caesars' Palace becoming very excited at the prospect of seeing Julio Iglesias and then having to listen to me for 15 minutes. I just kept reassuring them that Julio would be out soon and that he would be devilishly handsome.

When I arrived backstage, handsome Julio would always be sitting in his dressing room, dressed all in white and wearing his perfect tan. He would say, "Hello Rita, how is your life?"

"Great, Julio. How is yours?"

"Oh, my girlfriend is not talking to me," he would reply and continue reading his paper.

Ever since I'd performed in Edinburgh, British TV shows had shown an interest in me. I was flown over to appear on British talk shows hosted by Jasper Carrott, Des O'Connor and Terry Wogan. I'd also appeared on the British version of *Saturday Night Live.* An offer arrived for me to perform at The Prince's Trust show in London. This annual event raises money for various charities that are of a special interest to Prince Charles. It was not only an honor to be asked, but it was also an opportunity for Martin to return home and for me to meet his friends and visit with his parents.

Martin had cool friends, many of whom are in show business. I had already met Jayne Torvill and Christopher Dean and seen their breathtaking live show. Two other friends were cast members on that British version of SNL I had performed on – Hugh Laurie and Stephen Fry. Martin, Hugh and Stephen had been in shows at Cambridge together, along with Emma Thompson, another university friend who was beginning to garner notice as an actress.

I had never met royalty before and the instructions were quite detailed. The cast was arranged in a semi-circle an hour before the show. We were told how to address Prince Charles and Princess Diana, how to curtsy and bow, and how we should keep our answers to royal questions short. We stood in our formation and waited for the royal couple. When they appeared, we all stood up a little straighter. One thing about royalty: they have very erect posture. As the couple navigated the semi-circle, my nerves began to fray. What if I did something wrong? Would I be kicked off the bill? All of a sudden, Princess Diana was standing in front of me. She was even more beautiful in person and even her eyelashes had excellent posture. I performed my curtsy and said, "Hello, your Royal Highness," which I'm sure was incorrect. She replied, "And what do you do?"

I said, "I'm a comedian."

She said, "Oh. Do you mimic and make fun of people?"

I had been told to keep my answers short and I didn't really think I should go into my philosophy of comedy, so I just said "no" and she moved on.

Prince Charles took her place. I curtsied and couldn't remember what to call him so I said, "Hello, your Royal Prince Charles." He replied, "I hear you have married an Englishman. You have very good taste in men."

Impressive. He had taken the time to find out a little something about each performer so he could relate on a personal level. He was a real, royal pro! I can't remember much about the actual show, but

I'm assuming it went well. Martin also arranged a meeting for me with Jim Moir, the Head of Light Entertainment at the BBC, to discuss the possibility of my own six-part television series. I remember the meeting vividly. Jim got out a pad and pen and asked me how much stand-up material I had that would work with a British audience.

"About an hour," I said.

"Okay," he said, doing some division on his pad. "That's ten minutes a show. What are you going to do for the other 20?"

"Martin and I could write some sketches."

"Okay. Ten minutes of sketches. What else?"

"I could do a little film report each week about something crazy that happens in Hollywood."

"Like what?"

"There's a shop in Melrose Avenue that sells celebrity clothes after they're through with them. And a tour in a hearse that shows where famous people died."

"Good. That's 23 minutes a show. What else?"

"I can sing and dance. I was on Broadway."

"Okay, a song each week. Let's allow three minutes for that. That's 26 minutes. What else? You've got three minutes to fill once we allow for credits."

"At the end of my live shows, I take questions from the audience and improvise."

Jim put down the pad. "Three minutes of Q&A. That'll work. Done. I look forward to seeing it. We can film it in Studio Eight and I'll give you one of our best producers."

It was that simple; good old Britain, the BBC and Jim Moir. In the equivalent same meeting in America, we would have still been discussing what type of water I wanted to drink.

We spent the next four months back in Los Angeles, writing sketches, choosing songs and booking guest stars for the BBC show. One of my favorite activities is writing with Martin. We have the same sense of humor and can spend hours laughing at the situations we dream up. Access to Martin's famous friends' list was also a boon: Jennifer Saunders (pre-AbFab), Griff Rhys Jones, Jonathan Ross, Geoff McGivern, Philip Pope, Ade Edmondson, Helen Atkinson-Wood, Morwenna Banks, Michael Fenton Stevens and Stephen Fry all kindly agreed to appear with me.

Martin had sold his apartments in London and Melbourne. I decided to put my mini-house up for sale, so we could pool our resources. The new house we bought was on Benedict Canyon and was a two-bedroom, three-bathroom home. It was the first time I ever had more than one bathroom. I wrote to my friends in New York and said, "You have to come stay with us in Los Angeles and see our bathrooms."

The one thing I wanted to make sure of was that we could build a pool in the backyard. All my life, I had wanted a pool. The builder of the house brought in a pool expert who drew up different ways a pool could be constructed. We were assured that we could build a pool. We bought the house. I left numerous messages for the pool expert that were never returned. I finally contacted another pool company. This pool expert took one look at our backyard and said, "Which idiot said you could build a pool back here?"

"A pool expert."

"What exactly was he an expert in? There is no way in the world you can put a pool back here with that mountain in the back. A Jacuzzi would be a stretch."

So much for my pool fantasy.

We were busy writing the BBC show when I received a call to participate in *Comic Relief* on HBO. It was being staged that year at Radio City Music Hall in New York City, the very venue where I saw Liberace all those years ago. The day after we landed in NYC, Martin received a phone call that he was urgently needed in London. There was a problem with the Torvill and Dean ice skating show that only he could address. Martin was so looking forward to attending Comic Relief, and he didn't want to miss it. He informed his co-workers that the only way he could be in London and make it back to NYC in time was if he took the Concorde (I don't want to say he took advantage of the situation, but he always loved flying on the Concorde.) If you are a young person reading this, the Concorde was a narrow plane that flew across the Atlantic at the speed of sound and cut the flying time from New York to England to around three hours. Martin landed in England, had his meetings, the ice show went on, he got back on the Concorde and somehow was back in time for *Comic Relief.* Not too long after that, a Concorde exploded on a runway in France and now they no longer manufacture that particular aircraft. If Martin attempted that itinerary today, I suspect he would explode too.

It was lovely spending time with Robin, Billy and Whoopi, but the person I was most excited and intimidated to meet was Mary Tyler Moore. I have to say, she was as gracious and classy in person as she was on television and her comedic timing was impeccable. As with all of my shows, I can't remember what jokes I told. I only remember standing on that enormous stage and channeling Liberace.

Soon, we were back in Los Angeles and packing our suitcases for London. I think you can see why, at this time in my life, I didn't have a dog. That's not to say I wasn't acutely aware of missing the presence of a furry companion. I would embarrass Martin by petting strangers' dogs in the street, in airports, outside coffee bars and restaurants. He would mollify me by promising one day soon, when circumstances allowed, we would get a dog. Now, get on the plane.

We were to be in London recording for two months. Generous and sweet Jayne Torvill loaned us her house in Knightsbridge, one of the most beautiful areas of London, while she and Christopher Dean were out on tour. The house was directly across the street from the Knightsbridge Barracks. Every once in a while, I would look out the window and see horses on the balcony. That's a sight you don't forget.

We filmed the six episodes of *The Rita Rudner Show* at the BBC studios in White City in the spring of 1990 and had a ball. We left England before the shows aired, but our friends and family told us they were funny and the ratings were good. The shows later aired on a channel in America. I can't remember which one. I can only remember the horses on the balcony.

Later that year, I was phoned by Jerry Lewis and asked if I would appear on his MDA Labor Day Telethon, broadcasting live from Caesars Palace in Las Vegas. I shared a dressing room with Ray Charles, who had a braille copy of *Playboy*. I hope it was just the articles that were in braille. I didn't feel it to find out. Martin was standing in the wings, watching me tell my jokes to the small studio audience, when he noticed a diminutive man smoking to his right.

"Hey, this chick's funny," the man whispered.

"I know," said Martin, suddenly realizing he was talking to Sammy Davis, Jnr.

I have to admit I found Jerry Lewis to be a strange man. I admired him enormously for all he accomplished on behalf of MDA and I liked him as a straight actor; his performance in *King of Comedy* is a particular favorite. I'd never been a huge fan of his comedy films, but I could appreciate his skill.

Two years later, I appeared in the Montreal Comedy Festival and Jerry was receiving a special award. I was sharing a dressing room with Penn & Teller. Jerry burst into the room, picked up Penn Jillette's girlfriend and twirled her around.

"Rita Rudner. My favorite fucking female comedian!"

"I'm over here, Jerry," I said from the corner. "and that's a lot of fs."

Just then, the organizer of the festival entered the room. He explained to us that the show was on a strict timeline, because it was essentially a TV special, and asked us not to go over our allotted times. We all murmured our understanding and assent. The show began, and soon it was time for Jerry to receive his award. Loaded with self-regard, Mr. Lewis walked on stage and took the award. The audience dutifully applauded.

"They've asked me to keep it short," Jerry announced. "Your response has made that impossible."

He then did ten minutes longer than he was scheduled to do. He closed by hugging the award and tearfully telling the audience how much it meant to him. On his way offstage, he tossed the award onto the stage manager's desk. As far as I know, it's still there.

A few years later, he was asked his opinion of female comedians. "I don't like female comedians," he said, adding that he saw a woman, on stage or off, "as a producing machine that brings babies into the world. A woman doing comedy doesn't offend me, but it does set me back a bit. I, as a viewer, have trouble with it."

This came as a surprise to me, his "favorite fucking female comedian."

Apart from Jerry, I found that a lot of older performers enjoyed my comedy. I performed on a TV special celebrating George Burns' 95th birthday, which was a thrill. I still treasure the photo we took together and the 8x10 George signed for me – "Thanks, kid. Love, George." I feel privileged to have met and worked with some of the comedians that paved my way before they left us – not only George, but Bob Hope, Don Rickles, Phyllis Diller, Joan Rivers, Walter Matthau, Jack Lemmon, Carole Channing, Milton Berle, Jack Carter, Rose Marie, Alan King and, of course, Johnny Carson. Loved them all.

Despite my various TV appearances, Jerry Lewis was not the only one doubting the ability of female comedians. During our trips to Vegas, Martin researched the different show rooms that would be suitable for me to perform in as a headliner. The Copa Room at the Sands was the venue he decided would be the best fit. Martin and my agent, Steve, contacted the Sands. They were open to the idea of booking me, but said they couldn't possibly book a female comedian on her own; I would have to be paired with a man. Martin hired Jeff Altman, a very funny comedian, to perform in a double bill. The Copa Room was a venue that had a lot of history and much of it was still stuck to the floor. Frank Sinatra, Dean Martin and Sammy Davis (along with Joey Bishop and Peter Lawford) performed their Rat Pack shows there during the 1960s.

I had never stayed at the Sands Hotel before and was suitably impressed when Martin and I were shown to our suite. It was at the very top of the circular main building and was, at first glance, luxurious, with its floor-to-ceiling windows and balconies overlooking the Las Vegas strip. Upon closer inspection, it could have used a bit of updating. The pale orange carpeting and matching velvet sofa had what can only be described as suspicious stains and the plumbing sounded as if it had permanent indigestion. The plastic trees, however, were alive and in good condition.

Jeff and I were a hit that first Friday night and sold out the showroom. Exhausted from the drive from Los Angeles and the pressure of not knowing how we would be received, Martin and I returned to our orange sherbet suite. Now, here's something not a lot of people mention about Las Vegas. Everybody complains about how hot it is, but no one mentions the wind. It can be vicious, and it certainly was that Friday night. The windows rattled, the balconies shook and the circular tower swayed like it had drunk a few too many martinis. We felt like we would wake up in the morning and have landed in Oz. Jeff and I sold out the Saturday night show as well and, by the second night, Martin and I had more confidence in the hotel remaining on the ground.

A few months later I was booked at the Copa Room again. Jeff was busy performing in a television show, so this time I was paired with my old friend, Louie Anderson. Because of our previous windy experience, Martin and I requested a room at the back of the property. The Sands had a series of villas behind the main building and we figured we would be safer closer to the ground. This suite was a walk back in time. Legend had it that JFK had stayed there with Marilyn Monroe and little had been updated since then. There was a small kitchen outfitted with light green appliances from the 1960s, and a Formica bathroom decorated with plastic flowers draped over the shower curtain. There were three elaborate chandeliers: a huge one hung in the living room and two baby ones hung on either side of the bed. It was kooky, but safe from the wind.

Louie Anderson and I worked together numerous times throughout our careers. We were always given separate dressing rooms and end up staying together in one. For some reason, this dressing room doubled as a linen closet. It was quite large, but there were towels being stored throughout the space. There was also an enormous steamer in one corner. I can only assume that someone in the hotel snuck in late at night and secretly steamed the towels. Louie and I were the evening show. *Melinda, the First Lady of Magic* was the show at six. The first night of our engagement, I stood in the wings, while a curious selection of animals were paraded past me on their way home. The strangest one was a small horse with a horn glued to his forehead who, for the sake of show business, was pretending to be a unicorn.

Louie and I were also successful at the Copa. That night, Martin and I returned to our retro-suite, got into bed, watched a little television and went to sleep…. for about an hour. All of a sudden, the chandeliers began to shake and there were footsteps walking along the ceiling causing the bedroom to bounce.

"Martin," I said. "This is so weird. There is no room above us. What's happening?"

"I don't know. Maybe the ghosts of JFK and Marilyn?" he suggested.

The footsteps ceased and we went back to sleep. An hour later the same thing happened again. I called the front desk.

"Oh," the woman on duty said, "The rooms aren't up to code, so every hour a fireman has to walk the attic to make sure it hasn't caught fire."

I liked Martin's explanation better.

Louie and I were so popular we were offered ten weeks that year at the Copa Room. Martin and I were ecstatic. Financially, we were looking good. We decided to go back to Laguna Beach to look for a beach house to buy. Martin had rented a house on the beach for a while in Australia and it became a goal of his to have a beach house of his own. When we arrived at our hotel, we turned on the television to watch the news. A legendary hotel in Las Vegas, the Sands, was being readied for implosion. They must be kidding, we thought. This had to be an extremely elaborate practical joke. I called my agent, Steve.

"Steve, that was funny. How did you do that? I turned on the television and it said that they're imploding the Sands."

"I was going to tell you," he explained.

"But I have a contract," I whined.

"I don't think you want to enter into a legal battle here. I'll find you another casino."

It wasn't that the Sands didn't need imploding. In fact, they didn't need dynamite to knock that thing down. They could have just used a hairdryer. But couldn't they have waited a year? Martin and I had a pleasant weekend in Laguna and put our beach house dream on hold.

I have a house and I'm married, and I think you know what's next. I don't know if it's going to happen. I get such family pressure. My grandmother keeps asking me, "When am I going to be a great grandmother?" I keep saying, "I don't know. I guess as soon as you do something extraordinary."

I'm American. He's English. What would our children be like? They'd probably be rude, but disgusted by their own behavior.

Thirteen

Martin had friends from both England and Australia coming to stay with us in Los Angeles from time to time. One of those friends was Emma Thompson, who recently had married Ken Branagh. Ken had just had a colossal hit with his movie version of Shakespeare's *Henry the Fifth* (Hank Cinq as we all called it). He and Emma had finished filming their next movie *Dead Again* and were in Los Angeles and staying with us while it was going through the testing and editing process. Ken had a commitment to film another movie with the Sam Goldwyn Company and had a script he wasn't happy with. He had the time blocked out to film the movie and he had a location. He just didn't have a script that he liked. Remember when I told you one of my annoying sayings? "When the opportunity comes, you have to be ready? You can't get ready after the ...." I forgot how I said it, but you get the idea.

Martin and I had been dabbling with film scripts for years, ever since we rented that typewriter on the Gold Coast when we first got together. The previous summer we were in England. A friend of Martin's had inherited a castle in Yorkshire where we'd had lunch, and we noted at the time that it would make an excellent locale for a reunion movie.

We told Ken our idea of a group of university friends gathering together for a weekend in a stately home and he liked it. One problem: if he was going to switch projects, he'd need our script by the following week. Martin and I got to work. We presented Ken with a script seven days later and he approved. He began casting *Peter's Friends* the next week in England. As previously mentioned, Martin and Emma had both been in a comedy group called Footlights at Cambridge. Stephen Fry, Hugh Laurie and Tony

Slattery were also in the group. Phyllida Law, as well as being Emma's mother, was a well-known actress in England and Imelda Staunton was a talented actress and a friend of Emma's. All agreed to act in the film. I wrote the smallest part in the movie for myself because I didn't want to ruin it. Another part was offered to Alphonsia Emmanuel, whom we'd all recently admired in the British mini-series *House of Cards*. Ken cast Alex Lowe in the final part, a young actor he had worked with on stage.

Something you should know about Ken is that he has no fear. The four of us once embarked on a skiing vacation and went down the mountain perfectly in tune with our personalities. Martin waited in the bar until we came to our senses. I took a lesson and went down the bunny slope slowly with an instructor. Emma was somehow born an excellent skier and gracefully navigated down the intermediate slope and Ken, never having had any instruction, made his way down from the advanced slope in an improvisational style and, against all reasonable odds, lived.

Ken assembled a production crew and began filming the movie before any of the financing was in place. Sam Goldwyn wasn't happy. Movies are usually written and re-written by several writers before a camera is turned on. Sam wanted to give the script to another writer for what they call "a polish." There was a problem with that idea. Not only was the movie already being filmed, Martin and I had taken no money for the script so Sam didn't legally own it.

The stately home we filmed in was indeed stately, but it wasn't heated. We filmed in February and when one person caught a cold he or she generously shared it with the rest of the cast until everybody was sneezing. As the rushes were assembled, the movie began to come together, the financing fell into place and Sam Goldwyn began to relax.

As in most films, there was a bit of tension here and there. Looking back, much of it was our fault. Ken was the director and we were the writers but, in any film, the director possesses the ultimate power. However, Martin and I had been there when the pages were blank. We had some comedy opinions and were eager to share them. Ken was less eager to hear them. We were all proud of the end result, but our relationship with Ken never recovered. In other words, don't hold your breath waiting for *The Return of Peter's Friends*.

In 1983, Martin, Hugh, Stephen and Emma, already great friends from university days, had toured Australia together for almost three months and had developed a connection that clearly transferred onto the script and the screen. I felt very privileged to be allowed into that group and to work with such talented people. Martin and Emma had actually been friends since their London schooldays, and he has adored and admired her ever since. A year after *PF*, Emma won the Best Actress Oscar for *Howard's End*. Martin's reaction? "I'm surprised it took so long." Following her divorce from Ken, we were thrilled when she introduced us to her future husband Greg Wise, whom she met on *Sense & Sensibility*. Greg is a sweet, kind, gorgeous man and the four of us have remained great friends through the decades.

At first, Ken was surprised we'd written Hugh Laurie such a dramatic part. At the time, Hugh was better known for his comedic chops on TV shows like *The Black Adder*. However, Martin was confident that Hugh was primarily an actor, plus a musician, and there's no doubt that time has proven him correct. Stephen Fry is, of course, a delight and we shamelessly stole off-the-cuff remarks and bon mots made by him in conversation and stuck them in our screenplay. The other members of the cast were strangers to me, but we all got on so extremely well that my hardest dramatic job was maintaining my role as the outsider of the group.

The movie went on to win the Peter Sellers' Award in London for Best Comedy and was nominated for several other ritzy prizes. I won Best Supporting Actress at the American Comedy Awards, which sure as heck surprised me. The WGA nominated the script for Best Original Screenplay. It was successful in other parts of Europe as well as in America. My favorite part of the film was seeing Martin's and my name at the beginning as the writers. Martin's favorite memory is seeing a giant billboard of the film on the Champs Élysées in Paris.

About a month before we left for England, Martin and I moved again. One of our favorite weekend activities in Los Angeles was looking at open houses. It began very innocently. We just wanted to look at cool houses. Then there was this one house we kept going back to. Every weekend we would see if it was still on the market. Then we made an offer and it was accepted.

The house had everything we ever wanted: gorgeous views, cathedral ceilings, and, most importantly, a pool. It was larger than any house either of us had ever dreamed we would own and we owed more money than we ever dreamed we would owe. Martin was confident everything would work out. I had some sleepless nights. Working diligently for something and then finally attaining it can be immensely satisfying. Sometimes I would stand on our balcony and look into our living room and think about how lucky I was to live there.

Peter's Friends was a well-regarded movie and Martin and I were receiving calls for meetings with movie executives regarding script assignments. One of the first assignments we accepted was for a script based on a Lynda La Plante UK TV mini-series called *Widows*. When Martin and I read the contract, we were surprised at how many writers had previously been employed. Those writers' names were still on the contract. The movie company hadn't bothered to order new paperwork; they decided to merely cross the names out. The first name that had been crossed out was Lynda La Plante. Very often movie executives want a fresh take on the material that they bought because they liked it so much. The first sentence of our contract contained the words, "If you are removed from this project." Welcome to film writing in Hollywood! Martin and I wrote a version of the movie (for Bette Midler, Goldie Hawn, Cher and probably Meryl Streep) and were duly fired. The movie was finally filmed 25 years later as a gritty drama. Meanwhile, we discovered that we could make a very substantial living in Hollywood writing films that, more than likely, would never be made.

I was still traveling and performing stand-up shows, but most of our days were spent in our office overlooking the mountains. We wrote all morning, went out to lunch and swam in the afternoons. It was all going, shall we say, swimmingly and then, on January 17th 1994, when Martin and I were asleep, the whole house began to rock. At first, I thought I was having a bad dream. It was like being in a raging storm on a ship in the middle of the ocean. Our bedroom had a cathedral ceiling that featured wooden beams. I looked up and pictured the beams landing on our heads. I was sure it was the end of our lives.

Martin shouted, "Earthquake, get under a doorway." We stood under a doorway until we could make it out of the house. It was around 5:00 a.m. and burglar alarms and car alarms were screaming all over Beverly Hills. We stood on the street in our pajamas with all our neighbors in various states of shock. Martin stared at our crumbling investment and said, "We bought a new house and now we have a fixer-upper." One of our neighbors, whom I had never met, strolled up to me and said, "I always wanted to tell you, I loved *Peter's Friends*." As Martin and I stood on the street we could smell massive amounts of alcohol in the air. Almost all of the bottles of various liquors in the houses had inadvertently shattered and mixed themselves into aerosol cocktails.

One of our neighbors turned on his car radio and we listened to reports of the damage. The aftershocks continued for hours after the initial earthquake and each one brought us directly back to a state of panic. Martin and I decided it was time to enter our house and inspect the destruction. All of our French doors had sprung open and were now so out of alignment, they could not be closed. There were cracks in almost every wall. I tried to push the door to the kitchen open and something was blocking it. When I finally opened it, I found a sea of broken glass mixed with food. The doors to the refrigerator had blown off and were on the other side of the kitchen. The cabinets were hanging open and all of the broken dishes and glasses were splattered across the room. Upstairs, the cabinets in the bathroom were on the floor and their contents were scattered across the floor. The closet looked like it had been hit by an earthquake because it had just been hit by an earthquake.

There was no electricity and Martin and I were nervous about spending the night in the house. We had an idea. There was one house in the neighborhood that had an emergency generator and we could see the lights in this mansion glistening in the distance. Martin and I, plus a few neighbors, rang the billionaire's bell outside the gate of his formidable mansion. After a disaster, people are always inclined to ban together and help one another out. Not in Hollywood. Mr. Billionaire never answered his bell. He was probably too busy trying to clean up his wine cellar. Martin and I decided to see if we could secure a hotel room for the night. We ended up at the Four Seasons eating breakfast next to John Cleese, Walter Cronkite and Jane Fonda. Evidently, the Four Seasons was the place to be after an earthquake.

We were very lucky there was no structural damage to our house. The house next door and the one across the street were both red-taped and had to be demolished and totally rebuilt. Something very strange occurred in our house, though. The wires to the telephones were now behind the walls. Evidently, the earthquake had a vertical motion and our walls had briefly separated from the floors and the telephone wires had disappeared behind them. Patching up the cracks in our walls, repainting the house, re-attaching cabinets, buying new dishes, glasses and artwork wasn't cheap, but we had earthquake insurance. Hah! Turned out the insurance company would only pay us $200 for the contents of our refrigerator. Maybe my dad had been right about insurance?

Back in earthquake-free Nevada, the Sands in Las Vegas was blown up with dynamite rather than a fault line shift and the explosion was filmed for a Nicolas Cage movie (*Con Air*, I think). It was eventually replaced by the Venetian and the Palazzo, but in the meantime, Louie Anderson and I had done so well there we were booked into the big showroom at Bally's.

The Copa Room was 400 seats but the showroom at Bally's was triple that size. Martin assured us he would help promote it and make it successful, but Louie and I were both apprehensive about selling 15,000 tickets over a ten-day period. I used to wander down to the box office a few times a day to see how we were doing. One time I stood behind a woman who said, "I'd like two tickets to the show starring Loni Anderson and Reba McEntire." I hope she wasn't disappointed when Louie and I showed up on stage.

Martin employed a promotion he'd used successfully in Australia – he'd advertise Louie and me on the sides of a truck that he'd have driven slowly up and down the Strip. We were the first ones to do that, so blame us if you get stuck behind one of those trucks during your next Vegas visit. The show did so well that Martin added an extra performance on the two Saturday nights. He has always told me, "If the extra show is there, do it. Someday it won't be there." To this day, I never say "no" to an additional show.

One night the door to my dressing room was flung open by Debbie Reynolds, whom I had never met.

"Funny show, but you didn't introduce me!"

"Sorry?"

"When there are celebrities in your audience, you always introduce them."

I apologized. "Nobody told me you were in the audience."

"I'm performing next door at the Aladdin with Robert Goulet and Rip Taylor. Robert starts with "The Impossible Dream." Where do you go from there? You can't. This is a nice dressing room."

"Thank you."

"You know what? We should have a party in here. Like the old days. Get a piano in here and invite all the gang."

"Really?"

"Let's do it tomorrow night. After the show."

"But…"

"Bye."

And with that she was gone. Louie had been hiding in the bathroom.

"What was that?" he asked.

"Debbie Reynolds," I told him.

"We're on the seventh floor," said Martin. "How am I supposed to get a piano up here?"

"That's not my department," I said. "I have to round up the gang."

I decided "the gang" meant other headliners on the Strip. Diana Ross was appearing at Caesars. I called her. She sensibly refused to take my call.

"I have no gang!" I panicked.

"I have no piano," complained Martin.

And yet, somehow, by the next night, Martin made a piano appear, as well as a full bar. As for the gang, I figured Debbie might bring her own. Claiming a sore throat, Martin hid in our suite. After the show, Debbie arrived with Rip Taylor and an assortment of showfolk. Louie and I lasted for an hour or so and then disappeared. Nobody cared. Nobody played the piano either.

The following day, our phone rang. It was Rip Taylor, sounding apologetic.

"Debbie drank," he explained.

When I arrived at my dressing room, our security guard looked shattered.

"5:00 a.m." he croaked. "They left at 5:00 a.m.!"

Debbie the whirlwind and I became friends. She was great fun and went on to open her own casino, theater and show business museum in Las Vegas. She was resilience personified, until her daughter Carrie's death. That she couldn't take and she died the very next day.

Back in our house in Los Angeles, Martin and I wrote a spec. script for a situation comedy for me. A spec. script is a script that is written without being commissioned – i.e. speculative. It can end up in production or in a garbage can or, in Hollywood, both. At that time, stand-up comedians were being sought after for situation comedies because of the success of *Roseanne, Home Improvement* and *Seinfeld,* so our approach made sense. The script ended up in bidding wars between production companies and two networks. We were able to secure a pilot at CBS with Columbia as the producing studio.

We were proud of our script. The premise was a simple one. I played an advice columnist who was able to handle her reader's problems much better than those in her own life. We called it *Ask Rita.* We secured a good director – Andy Ackerman – who had worked on *Cheers*, and my supporting cast was excellent.

You've all seen situation comedies on television, so you know that not all of them are hits. The reasons certain comedies that aren't that funny appear on television are numerous. The writer could have a commitment. The star could have a commitment. The show that you are producing could be right for a time slot that is being vacated. Many things have to fall into place for a sit. com to air on television. This was not one of those instances.

The first thing to happen was the head of the network who had bought the show moved on to another job. This happens quite a bit in Hollywood and, when it happens, it is never good news for the shows that have been bought by the executive who has left the building. There is no upside for the new boss to hold on to the project. If it is a hit, it is the hit of the previous boss and if it is a failure, it is your fault for hanging on to it. There is also a tremendous amount of pressure put on a pilot. You are asked to produce a show that an audience will immediately become attached to. Often, it takes time for a show to find its audience so shows that have episode commitments have a better chance of succeeding than a show that just has a pilot.

Our show was funny and, while it is impossible to know this for sure, I feel that if it had been put on the air by CBS it would have had a better than average chance of success. However, the new boss had different ideas. He said there was only room for one new female-driven show on the network that year and he had the "hit." The show was called *The Five Mrs. Buchanans*. He was confident the show would be a winner because each Mrs. Buchanan was from a different part of America; north, south, east and west and there was even an old Mrs. Buchanan to appeal to the senior demographic. As executives say, "It tested through the roof." It limped through one season. Very often when you attempt to please everyone, you please no one. Testing can be deceiving.

THE
BONKERS
YEARS

We live on the outskirts of Beverly Hills. We're the poorest couple there. Everyone is rich in Beverly Hills. Really. I left my purse in a coffee shop by accident. I came back and someone had slipped more money into it.

Fourteen

Almost immediately after I found out that my CBS pilot show was not being picked up, I received the news that Bally's had a new entertainment director who decided that Louie Anderson should appear in the showroom by himself.

Bad news sometimes comes in threes. I hadn't been on *The Tonight Show* since Jay Leno took over in 1992. It is well-documented that Johnny Carson was intending the show to be continued on by David Letterman when he retired. In fact, the last time I was on with Johnny, I spoke to him during the commercial break and told him how much I and America were going to miss him. I was surprised when he leaned over to me and said, "Let's see how the new guy does when he has to do it every night." Johnny was obviously not ready to retire. I was aware a very funny but savage sketch on *Saturday Night Live* – the Carsenio sketch – had upset him. He had watched his friend Jack Benny be treated poorly by television in his later years, and Johnny was determined not to go that route. He chose to jump before he was pushed.

I actually like Jay. I had been on the show with him a couple of times when he was subbing for Johnny. He always made me laugh on his multiple appearances on *Late Night with David Letterman*. Jay was merely employing my old adage: "When an opportunity presents itself, be ready." Johnny had wanted Tuesday nights off and put Jay in as a place-holder. Dave had teased NBC executives and Jay had be-friended them. You could see clearly what happened. The fact that Dave had been the one to boost Jay into that guest-host spot in the first place by putting him on *Late Night* multiple times muddied the waters (Dave had always been generous with the old friends he'd started out with like Jeff Altman, George Miller and Jay).

I can't remember how often I did *The Tonight Show* with Johnny. I think there was one year when I did it eight times. If a guest dropped out on the day of the show, they would sometimes call me and ask me to drive over to Burbank with only an hour or so's notice. They trusted I would always deliver and knew Johnny liked me. Jim McCawley, the man who had refused to book me, had gone through an attitude adjustment once he realized I was a favorite of Johnny's. Now he was positively oleaginous and greeted me like a long-lost relative every time I arrived at NBC. I still remembered, "You're not funny and you have terrible timing." I forgave him, but I did once ask him whether he would consider booking me and Mary Lou Retton on the show together.

Anyway, that was then and this was now. My agent called the show and asked if they would book me. The news came back that I could be on, but I would be demoted to fourth guest. Now, I knew I wasn't a big star, but I had worked my way up to second guest and occasional first guest and would have been happy with third. But fourth? I didn't even think there was such a thing as fourth. Was I going to be on after they turned the cameras off? I called the show myself to try to understand what I had done wrong. Helen Kushnick, Jay's manager whom I had never met, took the phone call and proceeded to tell me, using very colorful words that began with "f," that I was lucky to even be on the show. I was a Johnny guest and Jay was going to have his own guests and as a matter of fact, they had just had a meeting with the executive in charge of the program and my name had come up as an example of what was wrong with the show. I hung up the phone and was understandably shaken. I can't remember if I even did the show or not, but, boy, I remember that phone call. I know I've said this before but I'll say it again: "If you rely on show business for love, you are going to be in trouble."

Meanwhile, the movie script sideline Martin and I had developed was gathering steam. We were commissioned to write a script for a married couple that Warner Brothers wanted to put together in a film: Tom Arnold and Rosanne Barr. Timing is everything in show business and back in the early 1990s those two were constantly in the news. All I can remember about the script's premise was that it was a romantic comedy set in Hawaii. Its title was *Trouble in Paradise* and the producer was Joel Silver of *Lethal Weapon* and *Die Hard* fame. We figured we'd made the big-time when we approached the studio one day and announced ourselves at the front gate.

"We'll pull a cone for you," the security guard announced.

A parking spot protected by an orange cone was in premier position in front of Joel Silver's offices. The cone was duly pulled and we proudly parked our A-lister car there. Thinking back, maybe it was Joel who had made the big-time.

Martin and I handed the script in and the studio actually liked it. We decided we would take a vacation as a present to ourselves. I had always wanted to see Venice and Martin wanted to show me the south of France. We booked the air tickets, reserved hotels and even had the car rented. Martin had a map of how we would drive through Italy into France. We then received a call that the studio wanted one more rewrite and they were putting the movie into production. They also wanted Martin and I to be available for rewrites on the set. Martin said, "We are going to be out of town." The executive said, "If you do that, we will hire someone else to rewrite your script." We canceled our trip and rewrote the movie. Then the studio told us they had gone off Roseanne and Tom. Could we rewrite it for Michael Douglas and Whoopi Goldberg? What?! We should have gone to Europe. Needless to say, *Trouble in Paradise* never saw the light of day, and we were beginning to get an inkling of how frustrating being a writer in Hollywood could be. I recalled how working in TV commercials had frustrated me in New York. This was a similar experience, except with more zeros added to the paycheck.

We were relieved, then, when Las Vegas came calling once more. Richard Sturm, the entertainment director who had previously employed me at Bally's, was now in charge of a new, vast hotel that was opening on the strip - the MGM Grand. Richard Sturm booked Dennis Miller and me to appear in their Hollywood Theatre, with Martin producing. Dennis and I had worked theaters across the country together and he and Martin had become good friends.

In fact, Dennis and I had already worked Las Vegas together in a double-bill at what was then called the Las Vegas Hilton. One night we were told Bill Cosby would be seeing the show and coming backstage to chat afterwards. *The Cosby Show* was the hottest comedy on TV and growing up I had been a big fan of *I Spy* with Cosby and Robert Culp. I was excited to meet him. Our show went well and I sat in my dressing room, waiting to be called into the green room. After twenty minutes, I ventured out to find out what was keeping Mr. Cosby. Maybe his fans were monopolizing him outside and he needed rescuing?

"He's already been back," the stage manager said. "He only wanted to see Dennis."

At the time I was upset, but given how events transpired, maybe I was lucky!

Working at the MGM was a fantastic experience. We stayed in the VIP section of the hotel on the 29th floor. The rooms were amazing: two floors with a full kitchen, elevator, jacuzzi tubs and, for added excitement, a butler at your around-the-clock request. There was also breakfast in the center lounge and sushi and appetizers arrived at around 4:00 p.m. accompanied by a chilled chardonnay. Dennis and I sold out the theatre and even added a third show on the Saturday night which Martin sold through a voiceover announcement in the hotel's many elevators. I'm not sure Dennis has ever quite forgiven Martin for the three-show-night!

Martin and I don't gamble, so we didn't have much to do during the daytime. On Saturday afternoon we wandered over to the Excalibur hotel to see a show called *The Sooper Dogs*. The show consisted of dogs from Las Vegas animal shelters that had been taught to perform tricks. There was one dog that caught our attention. His name was Bonkers. Bonkers was a big, hairy sheepdog mix that was the high-jumper in the show. He was also able to balance on a rope and howled along to the song "Happy Birthday" when it was sung to children in the audience. Martin had never owned a dog. Martin's mother never allowed an animal in her house. Once, her kitchen caught fire and she even made the firemen take their boots off before they extinguished the flames. Bonkers caught my eye as well because he looked so much like Agatha.

In between writing movies for studios, Martin and I had been trying to write a film script on spec. The spec. market was hot at the time, but we just couldn't think of an idea we thought might sell. Then, one afternoon after grocery shopping, I arrived back at my car to find a flyer on my windshield that read, "Beginner hypnotist needs willing subjects." By the time I arrived back to our house with the food, I had an idea. What if a couple hired a novice hypnotist for their pre-wedding party and he accidentally hypnotizes the bride into not knowing who her husband is and he can't undo it.? The groom has a week to recreate their relationship and make her fall in love with him all over again before the actual wedding. We wrote the script and it sold immediately for a silly amount of money. That was a terrific feeling. In the contract, Martin and I had to deliver two more rewrites to address the production company's notes. Eventually, the production company decided they didn't like the script they had fashioned and it was put on a shelf, never to be seen again. I told you, it is possible to make an excellent living in Hollywood writing scripts that never get made, but it was beginning to get to us. A few years later, Adam Sandler and Drew Barrymore made a hit film with a very similar premise – *50 First Dates*. I knew it was a good idea.

A few months later, Dennis and I were once again booked at the MGM. Martin and I immediately decided to re-attend *The Sooper Dogs* to have another look at Bonkers. We were surprised to find out that Bonkers was no longer in the show. We were distraught. Was there a new doggie entertainment director and had Bonkers been fired? Had he demanded a doggie raise? Martin said, "Go backstage and find out what happened."

After the show was over, I made my way backstage and found Stacy Moore, the creator of the show, and demanded an explanation. I had paid five dollars to see Bonkers. Where was he? The explanation wasn't good. Bonkers had somehow slipped out of Stacy's backyard and been hit by a car. His left leg had been shattered and he was no longer able to take part in the show. Stacy had arranged for a veterinary surgeon to place some steel pins in his leg and he was resting comfortably, but his future was still uncertain. Bonkers would probably have to be returned to a shelter. I immediately said, "We'll take Bonkers back to Los Angeles with us, take care of him and give him a good home."

Stacy said that Bonkers wasn't ready to be moved yet, but to keep in touch. I called Stacy every few weeks but Bonkers' leg was taking more time than expected. Finally, about three months later, Stacy called and announced that Bonkers was fit to travel. Martin and I drove to Las Vegas and met Stacy in the parking lot of the Excalibur. It went down a little like a drug deal, even though I've never done a drug deal. Stacy said, "I'll be in a white van in the south west corner of the lot. I'll be wearing a red shirt and a white cap." Martin and I spotted the white van. Stacy was waiting in the van with Bonkers.

"Do you have the dog?" I mumbled.

"Got him," Stacy replied.

Stacy exited the van and lifted Bonkers out of the rear of the vehicle. Bonkers had one leg shaved, revealing a long scar, and he was wearing a rope collar and leash. He was also missing some bottom teeth that had been shattered in the car accident. Stacy handed us a tin bowl along with the rope. We then had to sign a piece of paper promising the shelter that Bonkers had hailed from that we weren't going to sell him to a laboratory for research. We put Bonkers in the back seat and drove him back to Los Angeles. In anticipation, Martin and I had already purchased an over-sized dog house. We showed it to Bonkers and he would have none of it. He walked into the dog house, turned around and exited it in a dismissive fashion. We had also bought him some doggie toys. Nope. A tennis ball, however, was a big hit. I went out and purchased a collar and leash for our new dog and Martin and I took him for our first walk as a family.

Bonkers had lived in a yard his whole life, so naturally, he wasn't house broken. We had a large, closed-in patio in the front of our house, so his first night was spent outside, avoiding his dog house. Every two hours I would sneak down to check on him and he would pop his head up and look through the glass in our front door as if to say, "It looks really nice in there." It wasn't long before Bonkers was sleeping on our bed.

Martin and I noticed a few holdovers from Bonkers' former life in show business. If you wanted him to come into a room you didn't have to call his name. You just had to clap. He would immediately run into the room as if to say, "Am I on?" I had a hula hoop for exercise purposes. I took it out of the closet and Bonkers stared at it. I held it out and Bonkers jumped through it. His leg had healed perfectly and he no longer had a limp, but I still only held it a few inches from the ground. When Martin's birthday rolled around, I sang a feeble version of "Happy Birthday" that evening at dinner. Suddenly, Bonkers was singing along with me. Bonkers might have been retired, but he still had showbiz in his blood. That turned out to be fortuitous.

On the way to my next gig in Vegas, we were driving along the I-15 and I thought I would call Richard Sturm and tell him that we were bringing the dog. Richard said, "I'm so sorry, we can't allow dogs in the hotel."

"What?" I replied.

"It's a legal matter. If the dog bites someone, we can be sued. I love dogs, but unless the dog is in the show, it can't stay in the hotel."

We were around 20 miles outside of Las Vegas and I had to figure out a way to put Bonkers in my show.

Bonkers was greeted enthusiastically on the 29th floor. I think guests who had a few too many drinks might have thought they were hallucinating when they saw a huge, hairy dog bounding down the hallway, but nobody objected to Bonkers' canine presence. The show was at 8:00. Dennis and I rotated who went on first and it was my turn that night. I walked Bonkers down to the dressing room with me and asked the stage manager to bring him to the side of the stage at the end of my set and let him off the leash. I still had no idea what I was going to do with him. I was just going to ask the audience if they wanted to see my dog Bonkers. My show ended and I called Bonkers on stage. Being so big and hairy, he made quite an impression. He was wagging his tail so I said, "Bonkers, keep wagging your tail. Don't stop." The audience laughed. I then asked, "Ladies and gentlemen, would you like to see some impressions?" Bonkers was still wagging so I said, "Keep watching his tail. Windshield wiper, windshield wiper. Metronome, metronome." I then stuck my leg out and said, "Hit my leg with your tail." Bonkers and I quickly developed an act that worked every night. In fact, I once overheard someone asking at the box office, "Is the dog going to be in the show tonight? Good, then I'll buy a ticket."

Martin and I were becoming weary of writing and rewriting movies only to have them put on a shelf and forgotten. It was lucrative, but debilitating. We decided to write a script that we would keep hold of and not sell. I had an idea about an artificially inseminated career woman who finds out the identity and locale of her semen donor and travels to wine country to see if she and her donor might be compatible. Martin and I had taken a vacation with Ken Branagh and Emma Thompson in Napa and were surprised that nobody had ever used such a visually appealing setting for a film.

Finding the money to make a film is always a challenge. You can't get the money before you have a star attached and you can't get a star attached until you have the money. Martin and I seemed to have favorable reputations in the business, so we decided to cold-call-contact people we personally admired. I phoned Jack Lemmon's agent and he agreed to read the script and, if he liked it, he would pass it on to Jack. I did the same with Dudley Moore's agent. They all read the script and were interested. Richard Lewis was a friend of mine who I had recently made an episode of HBO's *Tales from the Crypt* with, and he said he was interested as well. Even though none of the actors were legally committed, we were able to walk into meetings with four names - Jack, Dudley, Richard and me - that piqued executive's interest. My manager at the time, Michael Rotenberg of 3 Arts Entertainment, knew of a new company that was looking for product. It was called Rysher Entertainment.

The movie was an ensemble and we managed to add Christine Lahti, John Shea, Faith Ford and the amazing Betty White to our cast. Betty White's agreement was a particular thrill for me, as Sue Ann Nivens from *The Mary Tyler Moore Show* was one of my all-time favorite TV characters. I'd also, of course, been a fan of *The Golden Girls*. Betty was just as wonderful in person as one would imagine she would be. As a comedic actress, her impeccable timing was so much fun to watch and work with. My only regret was that we didn't write a scene for Jack Lemmon and Betty White to do together. How much fun would that have been?

Martin was producing and directing the movie. Our first task was to figure out how to film the movie within the budget that we were given. Napa Valley turned out to be out of our financial league. Martin found a city called Temecula in Southern California that was a lesser-known wine-producing area. I phoned the city council and they put me in touch with a very enthusiastic woman named Jo. She had recently been put in charge of publicizing Temecula and getting it on the wine-producing map.

Jo showed us around the city and pointed out places that could be used in the film for little or no money. She was our kind of woman. Martin assembled a production team and we worked out of our house while organizing the shoot. Every room in our house was buzzing. Even the pool house was taken over by the production crew.

The accommodations we were able to secure while filming the movie in Temecula were perfect. We were all housed in small cabins that allowed pets. Bonkers was able to join us and didn't even have to go to work. Jack Lemmon also put in his contract that he had to bring his poodle. One of the great experiences Martin and I had filming this movie was working with a legend like Jack. He was not only a truly talented actor; he was a down to earth, good-hearted human being. We had a night shoot at an amphitheater that had to be filmed from midnight to five a.m. We asked Jack if there was anything we could bring to make the shoot easier for him. He meekly asked for a coffee maker. I hate when big stars have unreasonable demands.

The first day of filming didn't begin smoothly. One of the reasons I don't do movies, aside from the fact that nobody ever asks me, is that I hate to get up early. A movie day usually begins around dawn. That's the time we were all standing outside of our trailers because no one could find the keys.

Dudley Moore and I had many scenes together. This was at a time in Dudley's life when things were beginning to go wrong. I rehearsed our scenes with him over and over, but it was extremely difficult for him to remember his lines. Martin eventually had to film our scenes in pieces and at times have lines written in places where Dudley could see them. Being English, Martin grew up watching Dudley Moore and Peter Cook on British television and had idolized them. Indeed, Martin wrote a few monologues with Peter Cook and they had performed in a TV show together. Despite his problem remembering lines, Dudley was still able to give a performance in the movie that was unique and memorable. Later, his health problem was correctly diagnosed as progressive supranuclear palsy, and seven years after we worked together, he died at age sixty-six.

I had a problem working with Richard Lewis. We had multiple scenes together that were of a serious nature and he would always make me laugh. Richard can't help but be funny. At the end of the film I am on a stretcher, about to have a baby, and every time Martin said, "Action" Richard would inadvertently say something under his breath that made me guffaw. My director was not happy.

After the filming was complete (production), we set up an editing bay in one of our spare bedrooms (post-production) and worked with a wonderful French editor named Françoise Bonnot. Françoise was famed Greek director Costa-Gavras's editor and we were extremely lucky to have her. She had won an Oscar for *Z* in 1969 and had worked previously with Jack Lemmon and John Shea on *Missing*, another great Costa-Gavras film. We heard French noises coming from the room throughout the day. "Bah," "Noh," "Peh" were just a small sampling. After about a month we had a version of the movie to present to the executives.

There were two firm demands made by the president of Rysher. We wanted to call our film *Temecula*. He insisted that nobody would know what the movie was about and that nobody would be able to pronounce it. Maybe he had a point, so we changed the name of the film to *A Weekend in the Country*. It was bland, but descriptive. The other demand was that we change the music. Martin and I were huge fans of a female singing sister trio called The Roches. They had unique harmonies and melodies and we felt their sensibilities perfectly complemented the tone of our story. They had even appeared in the amphitheater scene in the film.

The Rysher president insisted there was no way he would release the film if we used that music. Martin and I had no choice and contracted another person to write the music. If there is one decision Martin and I compromised on and feel we shouldn't have, it was that one.

While *A Weekend in the Country* was in post-production, other films financed by Rysher were being released. None of them were hits and the company was running low on money. We tested our movie in Pasadena and, to our delight, it was extremely well-received. A second testing in Santa Monica was also positive. Martin and I were hopeful the company would spend some money on advertising. This was not to be. Advertising a movie is as expensive as making a movie and Rysher was not in a position to spend a great deal of money. Instead, our movie was sold to the USA Network and aired as a TV movie. If only we had known that in advance, we could have kept the name *Temecula* and more importantly, kept our lovely, quirky music.

It's a very transient place, Los Angeles. It's the only town where you can rent a dog. It's tough on relationships too. In Hollywood, a marriage is a success if it outlasts milk.

Fifteen

The house next door to us was receiving new tenants. The previous renter had been an Italian photographer. He employed fabulous looking women who sometimes showed up at our door late at night. I'll change the actual house numbers, but you'll get the idea. Our number was 4439 and his number was 4439 ½. See the problem? I was happy to see the photographer and his stunning models leave. Martin was less happy. Surprise.

I went next door to welcome the young couple who were moving in and it turned out that the wife was also in show business. Her name was Jennifer Lopez and her husband's name was Ojani. Jennifer was busily on her way to becoming JLo and Ojani was at home alone a lot. Not completely alone, though, because he bought two Doberman Pinchers. Suddenly we were living next door to wild kingdom. Every time I visited my mail box, I saw these dogs frothing at the fence. At night, Martin and I would be asleep and hear what sounded like a pack of wolves howling while they killed a pig. I had Ojani's number and would phone him and urge him to put the dogs inside, but to no avail. I began calling Jennifer on the set of her latest movie and begged her to do something about the dogs. She didn't appreciate it, but I had to try something.

Their marriage didn't last and it might have been a teensy bit my fault. One day I saw two moving trucks parked outside. One went west and one went east. The dogs went with Ojani. That evening, Martin and I had our first good sleep in months.

If you live and work in Hollywood, you're going to meet celebrities and you're going to be asked to perform for free. As I became more of a fixture in Los Angeles during the 1990s, I started regularly receiving invitations to various events. I was asked to roast

Chevy Chase at the Friar's Club in New York City. I was to be the first female ever to sit on the dais; a great honor, apparently. A roast involves insulting people and that's not my strong suit, but I always try to say "Yes" more than I say "No." I should have said "No." One of the objects in a roast is to be as off-color, risqué and vulgar as possible. Again, not my strong suit. Comedian after comedian took the podium and it wasn't just blue humor; it was navy blue humor. The thing about clean comedy is that, even if it's funny, it doesn't work after blue material. The impact will never be as great because the words that can be used in off-color comedy have a shock value that the words in clean comedy just don't have.

I could feel as I sat there and waited for my turn that none of the material I prepared was going to work. I developed a migraine. By the time it was my turn to insult Chevy, I had thought of an angle. I would swear, but do it incorrectly. I began by saying, "This isn't something I normally do but bear with me while I try. Here goes. Hello, f#####kers. Sh###t. How f####king are f####king you?" The first thing that happened while I was at the podium was that the roastee, Chevy Chase, got up to go to the bathroom. I said, "Hey, you sh###ty face, where are you the f###king going? You are a f#####ing, f#####cky, f#####kity head." I just continued to swear as much as I possibly could, even though I was making no sense. I got laughs through the three or four minutes but it seemed like an hour and my head was throbbing. Was this an honor? I didn't think so. The saving grace of these roasts is that all the money raised goes to charity, so it was worth doing, but I vowed never to roast again.

An invitation to celebrate Milton Berle's ninetieth birthday was a surprise. Milton Berle, the first major American TV star, enjoyed an eight-decade career in show business. I had never met him, but it was a very grand, formal invitation to his party and I was intrigued. It was held in the ballroom at the Beverly Hilton Hotel and Martin and I were seated at a table with the very funny Mike Myers and his wife. We were the only people there who were under eighty years old, except for Joni Mitchell. That's not a typographical error. For some reason Joni Mitchell was invited to Milton Berle's birthday party as well. I was looking for the ladies' room and I spotted Joni smoking in the lobby. I asked her, "How do you know Milton?"

She replied, "Never met him."

"Me either. I have no idea why he invited me."

"Me either," said Joni.

You see how much Joni Mitchell and I have in common?

The room read like a roster of "Who Was." Steve Allen was the host and, one by one, Red Buttons, Morey Amsterdam, Norm Crosby and many other comedians from the earlier days of television got up on stage to pay tribute to Milton. I still remember Steve Allen's introduction to Morey Amsterdam. "Ladies and gentlemen, please welcome the late Morey Amsterdam." Morey didn't care. He bounded onto the stage with the same enthusiasm he possessed as Buddy on *The Dick Van Dyke Show*.

A microphone was passed to our table and Mike and I also said a few words about Uncle Milty. Then Joni Mitchell got on stage, sang two songs and was completely wonderful.

While living in Los Angeles, I, like the majority of performers, participated in multiple shows for charity organizations. These shows are among the most difficult events to pull off. The producers are always well-meaning but very often the circumstances of the evening put the performer at a disadvantage. I think the one I recall with the most horror was my evening at the Playboy Mansion.

I had always heard about the Playboy Mansion and understandably had never been invited. This was a charity for a children's hospital and it seemed like an opportunity to see what was going on behind those gates and to raise money for a worthy cause at the same time. As we drove up, the gates parted and Martin and I pulled into the driveway. A valet took our car and we were ushered into the dark living room. I can only describe it as a place that desperately needed organ music. It didn't look like a place that housed playboys as much as it looked like a place that housed zombies.

The event was to be held outside and a giant plastic tent had been erected (excuse the expression) at the rear of the house. Martin and I roamed the grounds and witnessed various birds that seemed to be scratching. I might have imagined it, but I think one was applying ointment. There was the famous grotto, where all manners of activities were alleged to have regularly taken place, and young women who wore tight, short dresses and impossibly high heels were serving hors d'oeuvres and wine.

"When is Hugh Hefner coming?" I asked a serverette.

"Oh, he isn't coming. He's already asleep."

"He's asleep? It's 8.30. I thought he was a swinger."

The young lady didn't answer and continued on her way, balancing carefully on her stilettos.

I had not been informed that all of the attendees of the function would be older men. I mean, ALL. Many of them were smoking cigars, had been drinking for a few hours and had not eaten a great amount of food. I was not the act they wanted to see. I stood on the stage in the see-through plastic tent and began with, "This is the first time I've ever performed inside a condom." It got nothing. Not even a titter (again, excuse the expression.) I pointed to some of the young ladies serving drinks in their spandex minis, and said, "I'm not even dressed properly. No one told me it was bandage night." This time, the audience's expressions began turning hostile. I continued, "And Hugh Hefner isn't even here. I've been told that he's upstairs asleep. Let's wake him up. WAKE UP HUGH," I shouted at the top of my voice into the microphone. At this point, I decided that no matter what I did, it would be better if I didn't do it. I thanked the men for their generous donations and hoped they had a wonderful rest of their evening. I never saw the Playboy Mansion again, thank heaven.

Soon I was off on the road again, while Martin and Bonkers stayed home. I'd written a book of essays for Penguin Books and it was now ready for publication. I traveled to twenty cities and appeared on local radio shows and television shows across the country, doing readings and book signings in various book stores. During this tour, I was asked to appear on Bob Hope's last NBC television special. For some reason it was being filmed at the Columbus Zoo. I didn't ask why. I just went. Whenever I had the chance to meet a legendary comedian I always tried to be there, especially if there was also the opportunity to plug my book.

Bob Hope wasn't very well during his last special. His hearing and his sight were failing him. His daughter and I had a talk before I filmed my segment and she explained the situation. She said to be patient because the segment would have to be filmed multiple times before Bob got it right. Bob stood on stage and I went out to join him. It took him three or four times to say my introduction. Each time he recited the line the audience applauded enthusiastically. Once, he turned to me and said, "Can you believe I can get away with this?" Of course he could. He was Bob Hope.

Between takes, Bob asked me if there was anything I wanted him to say about my book and if I had anything for him to say. "Mom? Are you listening? Bob Hope just asked me what to say!" I actually wrote him a line that he liked.

The title of my book was called "Naked Beneath My Clothes." He said, "Rita, I hear you're naked beneath your clothes."

I said, "Yes, Bob, I am. Are you?"

He said, "No. Beneath my clothes, I have a layer of money."

I wrote Bob Hope a joke!

The book tour concluded with me playing Carnegie Hall. I hadn't been back to New York City for a few years and not only was it exciting to be playing Carnegie Hall, but I was looking forward to seeing my New York friends. Martin had one of Bonkers' favorite people move into our house to take care of him and met me in the city.

It was a truly special night. My dad flew in from Miami, many of my Broadway dancer friends attended, as did some of my teachers. Carnegie Hall is the one theater where my low ceiling theory does not apply. The acoustics are so amazing that the laughter bounces off the walls. Joan Rivers advised me to take the poster from the front of the theater. I did. Thanks, Joan. I had it framed and it still features on a wall in our house. My one regret of the evening is that when I thanked my friends, family and teachers, as well as the audience, at the end of my show, I forgot to thank my husband. He is so much a part of me and who I am and what I do, it slipped my mind. I told him that and he replied, "Good save." So, I'll say it now. Thank you, Martin

When we returned from New York, we discovered Michael Rotenberg from 3 Arts Entertainment, along with my agent Steve from ICM, had managed to arrange another shot at a sit-com pilot with CBS for me. This commitment was called a script deal. Let me arrange the order of network television commitments to make it clear. The most desirable commitment is a multi-episode, on-air commitment. After that there is a put-pilot commitment which means your show will get filmed. After that, there is a cast contingent commitment, which means the network has to approve the cast in order to get filmed. After that, there is a script commitment which means that if the network likes the script, it will get filmed. After that, there is no commitment.

What I had was a script commitment. Martin thought it best if he bowed out of this project so I could try a fresh take. The network picked another writer for me to write with. Her name was and is Wendy Goldman. Wendy and I worked so well together. Every day we got together was a day we spent most of our time, laughing at each other's ideas. We wrote a pilot we called *Dames*. It centered around three divorced women who lived together and were trying to restart their lives. Privately, Wendy and I called it *The Silver Girls*. Get it?

When the script was finished, we decided to perform it rather than just send it to the network and hope somebody liked it. Martin, Michael, Wendy, Steve and I set up a reading at the Laugh Factory, then a relatively new comedy club on Sunset Boulevard. We hired actors and actresses to read it out and filled the audience with friends and television executives. My dear friend Bob Saget, then starring on *Full House*, agreed to read the main male part. We arranged a lunch of sandwiches and sodas and even created a small set on the stage.

The reading couldn't have gone better. The script got huge laughs and trust me when I say, it isn't easy to make television executives laugh. Wendy and I were ecstatic at the reaction, as were the rest of my team. When I arrived home, the phone was ringing. It was the CBS Head of Comedy, relaying a message from the president of CBS, Les Moonves. He said, "Les felt there was a lot of talent on that stage. Unfortunately, we will not be filming your pilot. Bye." We couldn't have done a better presentation. I was beginning to realize a situation comedy just wasn't meant to be in my future.

Many people have asked me, "Why don't you do a sit-com?" It wasn't like I didn't try. There was always a guy like Les Moonves between me and the public, just as Jim – "You're not funny and you have bad timing" – McCawley stood for so long between me and *The Tonight Show*. I've concluded that a female comedic sensibility, particularly a subtle one, is not best judged by the sort of men who at that time were the arbiters of what the public got to see. The times seem to be changing, and I hope my efforts have in part contributed to the new generation of funny, successful women who are currently prospering. Sexism may have lessened, but now I'm battling ageism! What can you do?

My decades of success have to do with my live, direct relationship with the public. My shows go on sale, people buy tickets, I show up and do my very best to give them the most enjoyable and funniest evening it is possible to give them. I truly appreciate the fact that people get dressed, suffer through traffic, have to find a parking spot and sit in the dark next to strangers to see my show. That's why I always do my very best. That old saying where a comedian says to an audience, "Without you, there is no me!" is my truth.

Martin and I decided to try a different approach to TV. The E! Channel announced a plan to make a new series of half hour movies set in the milieu of show business. We thought of an idea called *Unfunny Girl*. The concept was that one veteran comedy manager bets another veteran comedy manager he can make the unfunniest girl in the world funny. In short, it was *Pygmalion*, but instead of turning a common girl into a lady, the manager turns a woman with no sense of humor into a stand-up comedian. I played the unfunny girl and Martin directed. We filmed it in Canada in January. It was a little frosty. I brought three coats and wore all of them… at the same time. The half hour featured Phyllis Diller, Jack Carter, Shecky Greene, Gene Barry, Frank Gorshin and me. It was a very funny set. Frank Gorshin arrived every morning looking like he hadn't slept in years. He confided in me that it was because he hadn't slept in years. He had terrible insomnia. Shecky kept everyone laughing by singing songs that always ended with, "Because I am a Jew." The movie aired on E! in a series called *Hollywood Off Ramp*, and we loved every second of the experience.

I adored Phyllis Diller. I remember Martin and I going out to dinner with her one night in Brentwood. The restaurant was very dark and Phyllis gifted us mini flashlights from her handbag so we could read the menus. Phyllis ordered soup as an appetizer. She had nearly finished it when I noticed one of her false eyelashes hanging precariously off its eyelid. As she took her last spoonful of soup, the eyelash descended. Our waiter whisked away her bowl and the eyelash before I could say anything, although "Waiter, there's an eyelash in my soup" might have been appropriate. As well as being very funny, Phyllis was also a marvelous pianist, a tremendous artist and a fabulous cook. One of her paintings currently hangs in my home. I was and am well aware of the debt I owed her as a female comedian pioneer.

Another female legend I enjoyed meeting was Carol Channing. Martin and I drove to Palm Springs, intent on convincing her to appear in a TV pilot that Showtime had commissioned us to write about a fledging fashion designer. Carol had recently messily-divorced, and was staying with a relative. As we approached the house, she was standing in the driveway, all trademark saucer eyes and toothy grin. She wasn't wearing her blonde wig, wore hardly any make-up and was in unbelievable shape. Hard to believe she was in her late seventies. She demonstratively waved her jewelry-free arms and hands at us. "I have nothing!" she screamed, cackling with laughter. We were treated to an afternoon of wonderful show business stories and gossip, peppered by pertinent comments about our script from someone who was very obviously a complete pro. At the end of our meeting, Carol graciously agreed to do the part. We drove back to Los Angeles and excitedly imparted the news to the TV executive in charge of our project. "Who's Carol Channing?" she asked. Unsurprisingly, that script never got filmed!

Martin and I were writers for hire (one executive eloquently defined a writer as "A Jew with a pencil") and the amount of ego subjugation the profession required was becoming more and more difficult to stomach. We were constantly expected to satisfy the whims, of the people we were working for. Nobody can ever be sure if a movie is going to be a hit or a miss. Studios pay hundreds of millions of dollars for a movie that can tank in a weekend. Networks pay show runners fortunes to create shows when there is no guarantee whether a TV show will find an audience or not. That's why stand-up is so liberating. If I write a joke that isn't funny, it didn't cost anything. The less money at stake, the calmer the surroundings. I think I just made up a new saying.

The last meeting about writing a movie that Martin and I attended took place at the Hotel Bel-Air at 7:00 in the morning. We're not morning people, but this particular producer we were meeting with was. The Hotel Bel-Air is situated in a fairy tale environment. It's in the foothills of Bel Air and as you drive up, you cross a mini-bridge above a gurgling stream. The birds are chirping and the valets are running. Celebrities are shuffling about and deals are being negotiated at the pool, the bar and the restaurant. Martin and I were seated at a table outside with this particular producer as he explained the movie he had in his head that he wanted us to write. We listened intently and finally I heard myself ask a question I never thought I would ask at 7:00 in the morning before coffee. I asked, "What exactly activates her magical powers?"

He replied, "I don't know. That's what I want you to figure out."

The report came back to our agent later in the day that he was not impressed with us and didn't feel we were the right people to interpret his vision.

He was correct.

There are both positives and negatives that accompany being a successful stand-up comedian. The positive is that you always have a way to make a living that does not involve pleasing another person's vision. The negative is that you enter collaborative projects knowing that your living does not revolve around that particular line of work. For me, the positive far outweighs the negative.

We went to the fights recently in Las Vegas. And I didn't know it's not just the main fight you're going to. It's all the preliminary fights before the main fight. The earlier you get there, the less important the fight. We got there very early. It was the Rosenblatts arguing about where to send their son to college.

Sixteen

Dennis Miller, Bonkers and I were again booked to play the MGM in Vegas. Martin and I were happily ensconced on the luxurious twenty ninth floor. I exercised Bonkers by running him up and down the hallway. I always enjoyed the looks on people's faces when I walked the big, hairy canine through the casino at eight in the morning to take him outside. The customers who had been playing the slot machines all night could not quite come to terms with what they were witnessing.

There was a new president of the MGM and I think you know what's coming. Dennis and I were still doing exceptional business, but our contract was up. At the end of our run there was a huge bouquet of flowers waiting for me in the dressing room. "How nice," I thought. Then I read the note. It was from Richard Sturm, the entertainment director. I can't remember the exact wording, but it went something like, "Thank you so much for your time and talents. Unfortunately, we will not be renewing your contract at this time. We hope to work with you again in the future. Sincerely, Richard Sturm."

I immediately called my agent.

"Steve, what happened?"

"It wasn't Richard," Steve explained. "It's the new president. He wants to try something new."

I'd worked for Richard for years and even performed at his wedding. Martin and I had an important decision to make. We could either be angry and leave in a huff or write a thank you note to Richard for all the wonderful times we had working for him both at Bally's and the MGM. We chose the latter. It was sad driving away from the MGM for the last time. We had no idea that it wouldn't be the last time.

Who would have thought that the end of my MGM contract could turn out to be a good thing? Not me, but that's what it turned out to be. My reputation as a successful comedian in Las Vegas had spread and I was finally hired to play the big casino showrooms on my own. Bonkers and I played the Monte Carlo, the Desert Inn and the Sahara. Bonkers was an easy co-star to work with. All he needed at the end of his performance was a milk bone.

Meanwhile, Martin had an idea. *Naked Beneath My Clothes* was a best-seller and I had also written a book entitled *Rita Rudner's Guide to Men* which consisted of tips about, you guessed it, men. That had sold well too. We had been to London and some of Martin's comedian friends – Ben Elton, Hugh Laurie, Stephen Fry, David Baddiel, Dawn French - had written or were writing comic novels. Writing a book wasn't as lucrative as writing a movie but it was so much more enjoyable. You really can't put a price on freedom. I decided to try a novel.

My literary agent at ICM – let's call her Sally Snit – who had sold my previous books, sneered at the idea of a comedian writing a novel and dismissed my sample chapters, so I fired her. Or she fired me. Someone got fired. Enter the best literary agent in Los Angeles, Alan Nevins, who began his career working for the famed super-agent Irving "Swifty" Lazar. Alan sold my idea to Simon & Schuster, and he represents my literary efforts (including this book) to this day. I don't know what happened to Sally Snit.

I write my act and essay books by myself, but my first novel *Tickled Pink* included Martin as an un-credited collaborator. He majored in English at Cambridge University and I majored in high kicks on Broadway, so I welcomed his assistance. We established a routine where I would write for a few hours in the morning, then he would read what I wrote and offer suggestions and make notes about changes, then we would have lunch and do something fun in the afternoon: swim, go to the movies, play tennis or indulge in our new guilty pleasure, golf.

While I was playing the Desert Inn in Las Vegas, the suite we were staying in overlooked the casino's golf course. Martin and I looked out and said, "Why is that fun? Why are they in those carts? Why are they wearing those funny clothes?"

One day we decided to try it. We had just seen *Tin Cup* starring Kevin Costner and Rene Russo and it inspired us. We each signed up for a series of six golf lessons at the driving range. Martin turned out to be pretty adept. I, on the other hand.... well, all I can tell you is that at the end of my sixth lesson, I turned around and saw my teacher walking away. He didn't even say goodbye. He just never wanted to see me again.

I'm terrible at golf, but I really like the cart. I like the scenery and I like that I don't care that I'm terrible at golf. The McCallum Theatre in Palm Desert is one of my very favorite theatres. I filmed my second one-hour HBO Special there - *Rita Rudner: Married without Children*. Martin and I bought a vacation home on a golf course in Palm Desert and semi-retired. We were still in our forties so it was a little early, but we needed a break from Los Angeles. There is something so relaxing about Palm Desert. My theory is that there is no ambition in the air. Most of the people who live there have already accomplished what they wanted to accomplish and now just want to hit the little, white ball into the hole.

It wasn't a big house, but it had a big view. From our patio we saw mountains that were tipped with snow and a lake that was surrounded by flowering bushes. Again, Martin and I would write in the morning, have lunch and take our cart out and play nine holes. I played the easy ones and on the par fives I just wrote down a score of eight and stayed in the cart.

Bonkers loved Palm Desert even more than we did. When the three of us drove up from Los Angeles he would somehow sense when we were nearing our house and begin to howl with joy. His favorite activity was sitting in the golf cart and waiting to be taken for a ride. At dusk I snuck him onto the course and he would run like a puppy.

As the 1990s wound to a close, I was beginning to travel less, although I was still happy whenever an offer came around for me to tell my jokes. New Year's Eve is my least favorite night to work. Audiences have had a lot to drink and very often they come equipped with horns and rattles. I have had interesting New Year's Eves, like the one in Las Vegas where I was booked to play two different hotels on the same night. The Strip is closed to cars and is absolutely impossible to navigate on New Year's so Martin and I mapped out routes through the back streets and alleys to get me to each gig on time. We practiced taking back roads from one gig to the other. We'd timed the trip. It was ten minutes from the Sahara to Harrah's, if you got lucky with the lights. Martin had said that if we were stopped by the police I should tell them that I was pregnant and my water just broke.

I ended my first show at 10:50 and another comedian took over. I played the next show from 11:00 until 11:50 and was back on stage at the first show at 11:59 to ring in the New Year. That drink at midnight was well deserved.

Writing a novel is quite a bit more challenging than writing essays. I was still writing my novel and performing stand-up when the year 2000 was approaching. New Year's Eve is usually a lucrative evening for performers but the night welcoming the arrival of 2000 was paying particularly well. There was a good deal of uncertainty surrounding the mysterious year 2000. What would happen at midnight? Would computers explode? Would planes fall out of the sky? Would VCRs have nervous break downs? No one was sure.

I had what seemed like a low-risk gig booked for New Year's Eve 2000. I was to perform in the ballroom of an upscale hotel in Palm Beach, Florida. I arrived the day before to avoid any planes falling out of the sky and was confident this gig was going to be a breeze. Since my father was living a few miles away in Miami, I invited him to the party. At around 10:30 p.m. on December 31st, my dad and I meandered down to the ballroom. Wealthy folks were having a swell time. There was lobster, caviar, champagne and the ice sculptures were of museum quality. I ordered my father a martini and I sat down and began crafting how I would begin my set. All of a sudden, the wealthy people began running out of the room. I wasn't sure what was happening but when I see wealthy people run, I run too. My father followed.

Then, I heard the voice over the loudspeaker. "Everyone must vacate the hotel immediately. There is a bomb threat. I repeat, everyone must vacate the hotel immediately." We all fled to the parking lot across the street while the police sirens roared towards the hotel. We waited there for a while and then I noticed that the staff was bringing the food and drinks into the parking lot. They were even bringing some of the ice sculptures.

A policeman came forward and announced that the squad had to search every room and stairwell in the hotel and we could expect to be in the parking lot for hours. The manager of the hotel asked me if I still wanted to perform my show. Martin had stayed back in Los Angeles but I still heard his producer-voice in my ear saying, "You always do the show. You don't get paid unless you do the show."

I said, "Of course I'm going to do the show."

There was a gas station on one side of the parking lot and the backstage technicians managed to have it opened so they could plug in a sound system. These industrious workers had assembled a makeshift stage in front of the gas station. There were no lights but one of the patrons had his car keys and drove his car to the front of the group and turned on its headlights. I performed my set to an unfocused but appreciative audience and counted down to midnight while looking at my watch. We were eventually allowed back in the hotel at around 2 a.m. when it was determined safe. The bomb threat was traced back to a disgruntled employee who had recently been fired. My dad never had his martini but was comfortably content drinking champagne with all of his new parking lot friends. Hello, year 2000.

Las Vegas is becoming classier. We have a ballet company now.
It's topless, but it's a ballet company.

Seventeen

One day, Martin and I were on the golf course in Palm Desert when Martin's cell phone rang. It was Richard Sturm from the MGM. An act had fallen out at the Hollywood Theatre, the theatre where Dennis Miller and I used to play together, and Richard wanted to know if I would perform with another comedian friend of mine, Richard Jeni. Martin said he would think about it and get back to him. I couldn't believe he didn't take the job. I had no other shows booked in Vegas.

I asked, "Why didn't you say 'yes'?"

Martin replied, "Because you've established yourself as a headliner and I think it's a backwards step being paired with a male comedian again."

I could see his reasoning, but a performer's self-worth is always wrapped up in their desirability and, at that point, I felt my desirability was certainly waning because I wasn't on TV as often. That one decision Martin made not to take that job shaped our future for the next two decades.

When we shot *Unfunny Girl* in Canada, Martin spent an hour chatting with Shecky Greene about Las Vegas in the 1960s and 1970s. Shecky revealed that one of his biggest hits had been at the Tropicana. The main room had been booked, so Shecky played the bar. Casino management placed wooden planks across the bar and created a makeshift stage. In a smaller room, Shecky had been a sensation and ran for months. Martin made a mental note. Everyone thought of Las Vegas as a place for headliners to play a large theater for a weekend to ten days maximum or for production shows that did extended runs. What if a headliner did an extended run in a smaller theater?

On one of our Las Vegas jaunts, Martin had spotted a small room that could potentially seat just over 300 patrons at the Las Vegas Hilton. It was open to the casino, but late at night electric-powered walls would descend and convert the space into a dance club. Martin had a thought: what if we lowered the walls earlier, put in seats and sold tickets? The casino bit and agreed to try it over a three-day weekend.

As we walked into the Hilton late Friday afternoon, there was a long line of people snaking through the casino.

"What are they lining up for?" I asked someone.

"The Rita Rudner Show," came the reply.

Word soon spread around town about our sold-out hit, and Richard Sturm called again, this time about a different theater; a smaller structure that ironically had been used previously for the Las Vegas branch of the Catch a Rising Star comedy club. The Manhattan club I had started in had proven so successful, it had franchised. The MGM was in negotiations with a long-running show from Paris called *Crazy Girls*. The negotiations were proving to be more complicated than they anticipated. The management had not renewed the comedy club's contract and they were stuck with an empty space smack in the middle of the casino. Would I like to perform my act there for a few weeks like I had at the Hilton and give the Crazy Girls a little time to stop being so crazy?

Few people are aware of how important advertising is in Las Vegas. The location of the billboards on which your image will appear and what that image will be can affect the degree of your success. Martin recognized the necessity of maximizing this opportunity. He went to work with the advertising department of the MGM to decide on how best to present me. It used to be called advertising, but now it's called branding, which always sounds painful to me.

There are few things I hate more in show business than having my photo taken, so instead of putting me through that horror, Martin raided the files of previous photographs. He came across an image of me doing the side split. I recall the photographer asking me if I could do anything unusual. I don't usually brag, but because I'm an ex-dancer, I'm limber. My hair was still partly in rollers and, clowning around, I said, "I can do this," and did a split. The photographer captured it. Martin found it in a pile and said, "This is a perfect horizontal shape for a billboard." I'm convinced that the image he chose was a major factor in my Las Vegas success. That, and, of course, Bonkers.

Driving to Vegas, I called the MGM and discovered we were almost sold out. Richard Sturm and Martin had renamed the space the *Cabaret Theatre*. Not only was the theater the perfect size, 400 seats, it was positioned in the middle of the casino floor and the rear of the theater was encased in glass windows. When I called Bonkers on at the end of my show, a group of people always flocked to the windows to see my big, hairy dog. The box office staff told me that some customers actually asked to see the comedian with the dog. Bonkers definitely helped sell tickets.

On my opening night, a huge bouquet of flowers arrived backstage. And I mean HUGE. It was from Siegfried and Roy, at that time the number one, biggest ticket-selling show in Las Vegas. I was beyond touched when they came to see my show on their first night off after I'd opened, and our friendship was born. A week later, the four of us enjoyed a hysterical lunch as we jointly opened the Las Vegas version of Wolfgang Puck's Spago restaurant. Siegfried was a worried pessimist and Roy was an energetic optimist.

"Every day I phone the box office," Siegfried told us, "and I think today is the day they tell me we have sold no tickets."

"Oh, she is such a silly old woman," Roy interrupted. "People love us. Of course, Rita, you are different from us. You have talent. You don't need no fucking tigers."

Years later, Bette Midler told me Roy had given her the same compliment. No matter; it was a good line. Of course, the irony of

THE DOGS

TINY

AGATHA

BONKERS

TWINKLE

BETSY

My mom, Frances,
up a tree.

The Rudners of
Miami.

My mom made me this tutu.

Banished to Camp GoAway.

Cyndi and I;
still friends.

Teenager desperate
to escape.

People happy to let
her go. My dad
with Dagny.

New York, here I am!

In Sondheim's *Follies*.

See if you can spot me. I'm the size of one of Tommy Tune's legs.

Career change.

With lifelong friend Julie and her daughter, Mackenzie.

Agatha and Tiny try to make Miami Nice.

Left: Martin and Rita in Edinburgh.

Below: Martin (still smoking) with Torvill & Dean, ice skaters who won Olympic gold with perfect marks.

Finally.

Tony Bennett.
Cool, huh?

Still playing tennis
together, a few
years later.

Right: George
and me. Above:
Bob and me.
Bob looks
happier.

Busy year. First Las Vegas.   Then London.

Bonkers in the Sooper Dogs
show, then transplanted to
Beverly Hills.

New apartment.
New baby.
Same dog.
Same husband.

My dad looking
thrilled about moving
to Las Vegas.

Molly looking
thrilled about
Bonkers.

Twinkle was
a better size
for Molly.

Things parents do for their kids. Snake, anyone?

Zipline, anyone?

Can we make it ANY bigger?

Making Barbara
Walters laugh
hours after my
hair fell out.

Meeting a
president while
wearing a wig.

A year later, and
I'm back! And
so's my hair.

Left: Mary Tyler Moore meets Jewish Tyler Moore.

Below: With dear Bob Saget and my other husband, agent Steve Levine.

In Hollywood, a marriage is a success if it outlasts milk.

People fleeing the comedy tent at the Latitude Festival thirty seconds into my act.

The Toaster about to meet its demise.

The cute but challenging London apartment.

Right: Hotel Splendido

Below: The 800 euro photograph. Should really have its own page.

The tennis years.

Charlene. Our last photo. We went
through six decades together.

And enter Dog #5……BETSY!!

the remark was unavoidable when just a few years after I'd met them, Roy was attacked on stage by one of his beloved tigers and suffered devastating, critical injuries. A couple of the shell-shocked backstage technicians from that show came to work on my show as S&R closed forever after that terrible night.

Not all encounters with celebrities were as easy-going as Siegfried and Roy. One day the phone rang in our 29th floor MGM suite. Martin answered it, as I was taking a shower.

"This is Mickey Rooney. I need to speak to Rita Rudner."

"I'm so sorry, Mr. Rooney," a surprised Martin responded. "Rita's not here currently. Can I help you?"

"Who are you?"

"I'm her husband."

"I need to speak to her. I've written her a song. It's gonna be a huge hit."

"Ummm…."

"Do you know who I am, kid?"

"I do. Of course. Andy Hardy. National Velvet. Ava Gardner. Sugar Babies. A phenomenal life. Congratulations."

"This song's so great."

"I'm sure it is," Martin vamped. "Couple of things…Rita writes all her own material, and she's known as a comedian, not a singer."

"Look, kid, when the Mick has written you a song, you take note."

By this time, I had arrived in the living room.

"Who is it?" I mouthed.

"The Mick," Martin mouthed back.

"Well, Mr. Rooney, I'll be sure to tell Rita you called. But as I say, she writes all her own material and doesn't really sing anymore."

"You don't get it. The Mick has written her a song."

Martin's short fuse had reached detonation.

"Well, the Rita will not be singing it. Thank you for calling, though."

My one month run at the MGM was extended to six months. I performed Wednesday through Sunday. Sunday night, the three of us would drive back to Los Angeles to sort out our mail and do our laundry and Wednesday morning we would drive back to Las Vegas to sold-out shows. There is yet another fact to be considered in my success in Las Vegas. In Los Angeles I was considered old news. I had pilots that had gone nowhere and there were new, young comedians on the horizon that were attracting attention. Las Vegas at that time was unfashionable - full of magicians, impressionists and nostalgia acts. O, the Cirque du Soleil show at the Bellagio, was considered novel and hip, but that was about it. I had numerous appearances on network and cable shows that had established me with the public and I had name recognition that was greater than many of the performers who were currently playing in the town.

In those days, the MGM had a theme park attached to its property. It was envisaged as a mini-Disneyland, but it was soon going to be replaced by high-rise apartments. One day we were wandering around the park before its scheduled demolition when Martin spotted a small theater.

"I've never noticed that before," he said.

It turns out the theater was used every couple of hours by an acrobat troupe who performed a free show. Being nosey, Martin also found out that a TV game show pilot had been recorded there recently. The pilot didn't get picked up, the set had been abandoned and it was still sitting backstage.

"I wonder if we could shoot something there with that set?" Martin pondered.

Eight weeks later I was hosting two pilots of *Ask Rita*. We took the idea we'd fictionalized in our first CBS pilot – me offering advice to strangers – and turned it into a panel show. I and four other know-nothing celebrities attempted to solve people's problems.

Comedians George Wallace, Jeff Foxworthy, Carrot Top, David Brenner and Pam Stone, together with actress Emily Procter and singers Sheena Easton and Susan Anton, kindly agreed to take part. Martin had involved the local Las Vegas NBC affiliate in the project and he edited the pilots in the local news edit bay. Now what should we do with them?

My husband and I, we keep discussing expanding our family. So far, we're either going to get a dog or have a child. We haven't quite decided whether we want to ruin our carpet or ruin our lives.

There's a plus side to having children, though. You've got to think of that. I don't want to be old and sick and not have someone to drain financially.

Eighteen

Eventually, the Crazy Girls sorted out their contract and my six-month run was seemingly coming to an end. But, not so fast.... At the end of my show, before I brought out Bonkers, I always asked whether anyone in the audience had any questions. One night, a question came from the audience. An attractive woman named Louise asked me if I could really do the splits like on my poster. I said, "Yes." She said, "Then do it." I replied, "You are a very demanding woman." I did a split. After the show, Louise and her husband came backstage. The husband turned out to be the vice president of the MGM, Felix Rappaport. That information is important because after my run ended at the Cabaret Theatre, Felix was made president of the New York-New York casino across the street. It was about one month later that Felix called my agent and inquired about building me my very own theater at New York-New York.

Martin and I were slightly hesitant. We loved working in Las Vegas, but living there permanently was a commitment we weren't sure we were ready to make. However, a very smart film producer, Lynda Obst, once gave me some excellent advice: "Ride the horse in the direction it's going." My horse kept heading up the I-15 and crossing the California/Nevada state line. On a conference call we asked Felix where the theater would be located. "I have a few ideas," he replied. "Why don't you come to the casino for the weekend and we could scout it out?" A few weeks later, we were walking around the casino floor with Felix looking for a suitable spot to build a theater.

There was a site behind the food court, but a fish fry restaurant was dangerously close and the whole theater could wind up smelling like trout. There were some convention rooms on the second floor that could be converted into a theater, but any time you are located on the second floor your chances of success decrease dramatically. We knew from the MGM that the location of the theater was supremely important. Then Felix walked us to the old sportsbook space. In Las Vegas, everything is constantly in motion and he had just moved the sportsbook to a location that was immediately visible when a customer walked in from the strip. The old sportsbook space seemed perfect. It was the correct size and, although not in the middle of the casino floor like the Cabaret Theatre, it was positioned on the right level.

Martin and I were just about to agree to enter the next phase of our lives when the room began to shake.

"What's happening?" I asked. "Is it an earthquake?"

"No," replied Felix. "It's just the roller coaster."

"How often does that happen?"

"About every three minutes. You can make a joke about it"

"I can make a joke about it every three minutes for an hour and a half every night?"

"You're a comedian. You'll figure it out," Felix assured me.

All of a sudden, Martin and I were back living in Los Angeles.

Then, the negotiations began. Felix really wanted me to be the headliner at his casino and was determined to figure out a way to, if not to silence the roller coaster, at least mute it. Steve Levine and Martin hammered out a deal and Felix began construction. At the same time, Felix tried to find a solution to the rattling, roller coaster. The first attempt involved changing the tracks. Great idea. Didn't work. The second attempt involved flying the original roller coaster architects over from Japan and replacing all the wheels. Nope. Opening night was upon us. The theater was built, Martin, Bonkers and I had rented an apartment for six months, the shows were selling well in advance and the theater was still shaking.

Martin demanded that the roller coaster stop running every night from 8:00 to 9:30. Felix was not happy. Upper management was even less happy. My show was a hit, but they were losing roller coaster revenue. Felix made one last attempt at silencing the uncooperative coaster. He hired sound experts who had a costly and uncertain solution. The pillars that supported the roller coaster extended directly into my theater and they were hollow. The sound experts suggested filling them with sand. This would absorb the vibrations and mute the sound and only cost about half a million dollars. I'll never forget a miserable Felix saying, "I wish I'd never had this idea of building a theater."

The solution worked and all the failed attempts were forgotten. Felix not only built me a theater, he also built me a fabulous star dressing room featuring pink everything. There was even a jar full of pink golf balls. Bonkers and I happily went to work at the new Cabaret Theatre every night. Ironically, Bonkers' favorite activity while I walked him to work was barking at the roller coaster.

I handled telling the jokes and Martin handled everything else to do with the production, particularly the advertising. He rented a huge billboard at the airport, so everyone flying into town would know I was on. Years later, one of our daughter's schoolfriends sidled up to her and said, "I know what your mommy does." "Do you?" "Yes. She works at the airport."

The casino's electronic billboards flashing on the strip are immensely valuable commodities. The restaurants, stores, casino events and other performers all jockey for position. Martin made sure I was prominently included in the rotation of events. I can't remember exactly but I think the order was blackjack, Gallagher's Steakhouse, Lord of the Dance and then me. One of Felix's darkest days was when he found out that with a pair of binoculars, Martin could see the electronic billboard from our apartment. He noticed that my advertisement was coming up every third rotation instead of every single rotation. Success, however, is a powerful deodorant.

We all got along great and strapped ourselves in for a fun ride. Later that year, Martin and I decided to sell our houses in Los Angeles and Palm Desert, as well as all of their contents. We purchased a fabulous three-bedroom penthouse overlooking the Strip. We were now officially Nevadans.

I've mentioned a daughter a few times, haven't I? Martin and I had been discussing the baby situation on and off the last few years. In the early part of our marriage, neither of us had ever had a strong desire to have children. We were too busy pursuing our career dreams and traveled too much. Now, however, we were in one place. Great, except I was already almost through my forties. A blood test revealed that I had a one percent chance of getting pregnant. I'm no mathematician but even I know those aren't good odds. Because of my mother's cancer history, I didn't want to try IVF. When Martin learned he would have to give me shots, he didn't want to try it either.

Ben Stein knows he is an actor, lawyer, speechwriter, political commentator and author, but what he doesn't know is that he was essential to Martin and I becoming parents. On a long flight back to Los Angeles from New York, Ben and I were seated next to each other. And he got me pregnant. No, that's not true. He told me how he couldn't wait to return home to see his son. During the conversation, he mentioned that he had adopted his child and explained how he went about it. I wrote down the name of his adoption lawyer, just in case Martin and I ever became serious about the subject, and stuck it in my messy wallet.

A few months later, Martin and I were discussing how old we were both getting, especially me (Martin is three years, four months and six days younger, but who's counting?) We decided to give the lawyer a call. I don't want to go into too much detail here, because I don't want to invade anybody's privacy, but I can give you the outline of our experience.

After contacting the lawyer, we set up a phone line that was to be exclusively used for the adoption process. Martin made up a brochure depicting who we were; it told a prospective birth mother why we wanted to adopt a baby and why we thought we would be good parents. The plan was that when the phone rang, we would answer it, talk to the expectant mother and everyone involved would decide whether it might be a good fit. If the answer was affirmative, we would send off the brochure and wait to see if we were the right parents in the expectant mother's opinion.

Weeks went by and the phone refused to ring. I called the phone from my friend's house and had Martin answer it just to make sure it was working. I contacted our lawyer and he said, "Sometimes this happens right away and sometime it takes years." Not very encouraging. A few months later the phone finally rang. It was a wrong number. Only kidding. Hey, I'm a comedian. On the other end of the phone was the woman who would eventually change our lives forever.

After chatting for a while, I asked if I could send her our parental brochure. She agreed. After a nervous few weeks she called back and wanted to meet us. She said she thought we would be extremely good parents and she was also very anxious to meet Bonkers. Martin and I owed a lot to this big, hairy mixed breed we had met in a parking lot ten years earlier.

Martin and I left the hospital five months later with a baby girl. I still remember in great detail taking Molly home. Here's something that happened that is ridiculous. For some reason, I had to sit in a wheelchair holding Molly and a nurse had to push me through the exit. I kept insisting I wasn't the person who had been through childbirth. The nurse explained that it was hospital protocol and pushed me through the doors. I handed Molly to Martin and prepared the car seat. After strapping our precious baby in, she closed her eyes and her head fell sideways. I screamed, "I've killed her." Molly opened her eyes and I realized she had only fallen asleep. I had a lot to learn.

We brought Molly home to her pink room with "Good Golly Miss Molly" painted on one wall. Molly was the first baby ever to bless the complex we now lived in. People would ask me why I chose to bring up a child in Las Vegas. Well, bizarrely, it was the one place I could both continue my career and be a mother. I could be with my family all day, go to work at 7:00 at night and be home before 10:00. You have to admit, those are pretty good hours.

Felix Rappaport wanted another show in my theatre as well as mine. Las Vegas management is all about maximization. Felix couldn't bear the thought that the beautiful theater he'd built was only being used two hours a day. Martin tried to dissuade him.

"When do you go home, Felix?"

"About 6:00pm."

"Your office is empty all night?"

"Yes."

"Why don't you put in a bed and rent it out for somebody to sleep there?" Martin asked facetiously.

Felix was unamused, and to keep him mollified Martin quickly wrote a show called *BOO!* It was a collection of funny, scary sketches and songs that could play after my show. Tickets would include a midnight ride on the roller coaster. Martin had seen an improvisational group in Los Angeles called Impro Theatre he liked, and he invited them to both perform and have input in the show under his direction. *BOO!* began the week after Molly was born and the cast became our good friends. It ran successfully for two years, which pleased Felix who, as far as I know, never rented out his office overnight, but I suspect he thought about it.

Just as we were settling into life with baby, we received a phone call from our local NBC affiliate station. Litton, a TV syndication company, had watched our *Ask Rita* pilots and wanted to try to syndicate a daytime series on American TV. We knew the odds were against us. Litton was a tiny company and would be going against the Hollywood studio monoliths – Universal, Paramount, Fox, Disney, Sony etc. However, we decided to give it a go. We would have to finance the production costs ourselves, and Litton would try to raise as much advertising revenue as possible minus its fee.

Over the next year or so, Martin and I made over 100 episodes of *Ask Rita*. To keep costs down, Martin shot the show like a game show rather than a talk show – i.e. five a day. A lot of my show business friends agreed to appear – Steve Martin, Paul Rodriguez, Dennis Miller, DL Hughley, Howie Mandel, Leeza Gibbons, Estelle Harris, David Brenner, Kevin Nealon, Cindy Margolis, Gena Lee Nolin, Sheena Easton, Jackée Harry, Joan Severance, Sinbad, Jeff Garlin, Teri Garr, Phyllis Diller, Rhonda Shear, Cheryl Hines, Connie Stevens, Rachael Harris and Heidi Fleiss are some of the people I remember agreeing to play with us. Also, the *BOO!* cast shot a few episodes with me as well. Plus, I sometimes ventured out to a special event or a show with a local crew and filmed a segment. Martin first edited the show in our apartment's TV room and then in the local NBC news editing booth, before transporting the tapes to a company so they could be sent out by satellite. Some stations couldn't receive the show by satellite, so we Fed-Exe'd tapes. It was a real mom'n'pop operation!

Litton did a terrific job, but we ended up in bad time slots on good stations and good time slots on bad stations. However, we did get 95% coverage of the country, which in itself was a victory. TBS bought re-runs of the show but aired them at 5:30 in the morning! Nevertheless, an organization called The Alliance of Women in Media Foundation chose to give me a Gracie Award (named after Gracie Allen) for Best Host, which was a gratifying acknowledgment of the show's existence. It was fun tilting at the windmill of television, but when we started to tire of the considerable effort involved, Litton and ourselves mutually agreed to retire the show.

We knew Steve Martin through Martin's friends, film director and writer Jonathan Lynn and his lovely psychotherapist wife Rita Lynn. Jonathan had directed Steve in *Bilko*. Steve was chosen to host that year's Oscars, and he asked if I would help write his opening monologue. I was nervous.

"I've never written for anyone but me before."

"It's very easy, Rita," Steve explained. "You write jokes as though they're for you, and then you give them to me."

In exchange, Steve agreed to appear on our little mom'n'pop TV show *Ask Rita*. I'm eternally grateful to him for agreeing to do it. He helped me out again after 9/11. I didn't perform that night. It just felt entirely inappropriate. However, the casino pressured me to perform the following night. I asked Steve for advice, and he convinced me that people needed to laugh and that I should go on. It was the right call.

When our daughter learned to walk, we totally child-proofed the house. She got in anyway.

Her favorite game was "Hide and Seek." It was my favorite game too. I didn't look for her right away.

Nineteen

Kids surprise you constantly. I used to count out loud while going through a tunnel on our way to Gymboree when Molly was about 16 months old. I didn't know whether I was getting through to her at all, I just did it. One day, we were in the car and I said, "One, two," and I heard a little voice in the back seat say, "Three, four." Glorious!

Another day, I was leaving Gymboree with Molly and I placed her in her car seat and was about to drive away. I heard a little voice in the back say, "Straps."

I had forgotten to buckle her in. It was a glimpse into the many things she would be telling me I was doing wrong in the years to come.

We were slightly apprehensive about Bonkers and how he would feel about a new baby in the house. You hear all sorts of nightmare scenarios featuring dogs attacking the babies when the parents aren't looking. We didn't have to worry about that. We had to worry about Molly attacking the dog. She never really took to Bonkers. She pulled his hair, she slapped him; once she hit him with a bag of walnuts. Bonkers would just stare at her and wonder what the heck she thought she was doing.

Believe it or not, parts of Las Vegas are relatively normal. Molly's elementary school was ordinary; however, some of the children were dropped off in the morning by trapeze. It was the only time I'd ever seen a playground with a stripper's pole. The math teacher only taught them to count to twenty-one. We tipped the English teacher to get a desk down front. There, I'm glad I got those jokes out of my system.

It was a perfect lifestyle. I could be a wife and mother during the day and Bonkers and I could be in show business at night. We were working six nights a week, my shows were selling out, friends and celebrities were dropping by to catch my act and Martin and I had become fast-friends with other Las Vegas headliners and performers. However, at Molly's school, I was just Molly's mom. One particular father always stood next to me when we were picking up our kids as our two girls often played together. After about six months, he said to me, "You know, I heard a rumor that Rita Rudner's kid goes to this school, but I've never seen her here."

"She probably makes the nanny pick the child up," I told him. "You know these showbiz types."

The only slight negative about Las Vegas was the weather. Have I mentioned that Vegas gets toasty in the summer? When Molly was about three, we decided to take a week off in August and go on a vacation. I realized we had never been on a vacation. The only time I travelled was for work. Our idea of a vacation was staying home. We had a friend look after Bonkers and the three of us drove to Laguna Beach. We stayed at the Montage Hotel, had drinks by the pool and I didn't go to work at night. I couldn't believe that I was actually one of those people who had a husband and a child and was getting dressed up in the evening to go to dinner rather than to do my show. Laguna was where we'd had our honeymoon and we still hoped to one day own a beach house in the area. We just had to get back to Vegas and continue saving money.

Martin and I are both only children so, of course, the responsibility of caring for our aging parents fell solely upon our shoulders. Martin moved his parents from London to Las Vegas so they could be a part of their granddaughter's life and I moved my dad from Miami. We built a house for Kay and Arthur and moved my dad Abe into an apartment in our high-rise complex.

One of the more entertaining, and indeed scary, aspects of my dad's move was unpacking the boxes that preceded him. He was never a logical parent, but I didn't expect to find cans of expired pineapple juice and baked beans. My dad had likewise packed dozens of boxes of Kleenex, laxatives, toothpaste and bottles of rubbing alcohol. My pathologically lazy father hadn't bothered to remove his clothes from their rusty hangers, and they were so dusty they were actually crunchy. We tossed the expired cans of food and replaced them with items that were more current. We bought him new clothes. We furnished the apartment and attempted to turn it into a cozy environment. I didn't think taking care of my dad was going to be easy, but I could never have anticipated the adventures that lay before me.

He exited the plane drunk. We had flown him first class and the free martinis had proven to be a little too enticing. The good news was that he seemed to love the apartment and for the first few months the move seemed to be a good idea. I brought Molly and Bonkers over a few times a week. We took him for breakfast every Sunday morning and once in a while he accompanied Bonkers and me to my show at New York-New York.

One Sunday breakfast, we were all sitting at the table and my father refused to remove his sunglasses.

"Dad, we're indoors. Take off your sunglasses."

"No," he replied.

"Why not?"

"Leave me alone. I like my sunglasses," he retaliated.

"Now I'm going to insist because I think something is wrong. Take off your glasses," I demanded.

My dad slowly removed his glasses to reveal two enormous black eyes.

"What happened?"

"I don't like having to say hello to the doorman when I go downstairs and I went out the back door and I don't see so well and a few days ago I tripped and fell over."

"This is all because you don't want to say 'hello'?"

"Yes. I don't want to have to say hello."

"Don't say hello. Just walk out of the building. Maybe wave."

"I'll try waving. But I don't want to."

My dad's life became even more exciting when he discovered a Walgreens within walking distance. I would be driving Molly home from school and see my dad shuffling along the sidewalk with bags full of boxes of Kleenex. I figured if the hoarding made him happy, I would let him continue until I got a complaint from Walgreens.

Eventually, the distractions wore off and depression began to set in. My father never really had the ability to focus on anyone but himself. The results of that state of mind can only lead to one thing: disappointment. As he sailed past 80, his eyesight failing and his physically abilities deteriorating, he could only dwell on his deficiencies. The fact that he had a happily married daughter, a healthy grandchild and an adorable family dog didn't enter into his consciousness. I took him to a doctor and had anti-depressants prescribed, but they didn't seem to help.

It was New Year's Day 2005 when I called my dad to see if he was ready to go to breakfast. There was no answer. I waited for 15 minutes and called again. Still no answer. I had a bad feeling. I asked Martin to accompany me to the apartment. I put the key in the lock and slowly pushed open the door.

"Dad? Dad?"

"I'm in the bathroom…" he replied.

"Thank heaven. I was worried about you!"

"…trying to commit suicide."

"What???!!!"

"Don't come in. I'm committing suicide."

Martin said, "I'll go in. You call 911."

Martin walked into the bathroom and I heard him lament "Oh, Abe, what have you done?"

Meanwhile, I found myself saying into a phone, "Hello, my father is in the bathtub trying to commit suicide. What do I do?"

The calm voice on the other end replied, "Don't let the water out of the tub. That increases the blood flow."

I yelled, "Martin, don't let the water out of the tub."

"Got it. Putting the plug back in now."

I waited outside in the living room until the ambulance arrived. I am so thankful that I never had to see the actual event and that the image is absent from my mental hard drive.

The paramedics entered the bathroom and my father was uncooperative.

"Don't touch me. I'm trying to commit suicide," he proclaimed.

A paramedic explained, "Either you let us take you out of the bath voluntarily or your daughter will see you being taken out in handcuffs. Your choice."

They taped up his wrists, lifted my dad out of the bath and placed him on a stretcher. Bizarrely, he was wearing a wet, grey sweatsuit. I rode with him in the back of the ambulance to the hospital. He never said a word to me the whole trip. The paramedic explained that my father was going to be fine because he had slit his wrists the wrong way: horizontally instead of vertically. That was an informative fact I never had reason to learn.

Martin met us at the hospital and my father was taken into the emergency room. When he finally spoke, it was apparent my father was furious. He barked at me via the doctor, "Why didn't you let me kill myself? Why did you have to stop me?"

"Calm down, Mr. Rudner," the doctor suggested.

"OK, then just let me go back home. I promise I won't do this again."

"That's not possible. We're going to have to get you mentally evaluated."

"I told you. I was a little crazy. I won't do this again."

The doctor explained that my father would have to be transferred to a mental hospital for at least 72 hours. He would be evaluated and then released.

"Does he live with you?" the doctor inquired.

"No, he has his own apartment."

"What floor?"

"Sixteenth."

"He's not going back there!" the doctor decreed.

It was January 1st and we had just signed a year's renewal on the lease, but that was the least of our problems.

The next afternoon, Martin and I made a trip to the mental hospital. My father was in good spirits. He had already made friends. He had mentioned to a woman in the facility that his daughter was a famous comedian in Las Vegas and, upon meeting me, the woman pulled out a camera and began taking photos. Evidently, this wasn't allowed and a skirmish ensued while a care-giver tried to take away the woman's camera. Just another calm, peaceful afternoon with my father.

I found a senior care facility that would take my dad on the condition he not try to attempt suicide again. As I unpacked his bags, I carefully took away any sharp objects: nail files, scissors, pencils and pens were all forbidden. Then, at the bottom of his suitcase, I found a picture of me in a frame. The glass was smashed into pieces.

"Dad, what's this?" I asked.

"Okay, take it," he replied, defeated. "Rita Carol, is there any way you can get me to Sweden? I think you're allowed to kill yourself there."

"Dad, you don't have a passport."

"Get me one," he demanded.

"I'm not going to get you a passport and pay for a ticket to Sweden so you can kill yourself."

"Then can you get me some pills and I'll do it here?" he asked.

"No. I'm not Dr. Kevorkian."

"Do you know him?"

"No, and even if I did, this is a ridiculous conversation. Do you want me to go to prison for the rest of my life for killing my father?"

"Okay, Okay. I was just asking. Jeez."

This was a verbatim conversation I had with my father.

He never tried to kill himself by slitting his wrists again. He tried to do it by starving himself. I attempted to reason with him. I even showed up to have lunch with him. One of my favorite moments was when we went to sit at a table and he said, "I don't want to sit next to that woman. She has a cold."

Here was a man who was trying to kill himself who didn't want to catch a cold. I told you; logic was never his strong point. My father was eventually kicked out of the facility for refusing to eat. He was transferred to the mental ward of another hospital. That evening, I received a call.

"Hello, I'm Dr. so and so. Your father is refusing to eat. We have two choices. We can insert a tube into his stomach or we can administer shock therapy to try to reprogram him."

At this point, I'm afraid I lost it.

"Put my father on the phone now!!" I demanded.

"Listen, Dad, I've done everything I can do for you. I've supported you for the last 25 years. I've moved you to Las Vegas. I've rented you an apartment. I've done your grocery shopping. I've visited you faithfully with my family. All I'm asking you to do, you selfish bastard, is chew!!!! That's all you have to do. Eat food. That's it. That's all you have to do."

"Okay, I'll eat," he replied, shocked. "No need to get angry."

The doctor called me the next day. "I don't know what you did, but he's eating. If he continues eating for the next few days, we can release him."

That was the good news, the bad news was, there was no place to put him. I called one of his psychiatrists to ask their advice.

"Was he ever in the army?" she asked.

"Yes. He fought on the beaches of New Jersey," I replied.

"Then the veterans' home has to take him."

As luck would have it, all the records of my father's service had been destroyed in a fire a long time ago. Martin and I wouldn't give up. We dug up some pictures of him in uniform and met with the facility's administrator. After intense begging, they agreed to admit him.

We visited my dad every week and even brought Bonkers who dutifully jumped on his bed and tried to lick him. My father exhibited no sense of enjoyment or appreciation of anything we were doing for him. He was still angry that he hadn't been allowed to commit suicide. About a month after he entered the veteran's home, I received a call that my father had died during the night. I never asked what caused his death. It didn't really matter. Honestly, it was as much of a relief to me as it was to him. There are so many people who have parents who die too soon. My mom died way too soon. I still feel that loss deeply and know I always will. I have different feelings about my father.

As long as we're on a bit of a downer, here comes another one. The only thing that's wrong with dogs is that they get old. By my fourth year at New York-New York, Bonkers wasn't arriving on stage with the same bounce. It was time for him to retire. He had worked at The Riviera, The Monte Carlo, The Desert Inn, The MGM and New York-New York. Quite a resumé for a dog. I still took him to the show every night at New York-New York because he would wait for me at the front door and I didn't want to disappoint him, but his performing days were over. One day while Martin and I were eating lunch we heard a strange cough coming from Bonkers. Martin and I looked at each other and we both knew something was seriously wrong. We rushed him to the vet and were told to leave him there overnight. It was the first night Bonkers hadn't accompanied me to the casino. The next morning Martin called to receive the diagnosis. I wasn't brave enough.

The vet explained that Bonkers had water in his lungs. We had a choice. We could have him put to sleep or try a regimen of pills and see how he responded. We chose the pills. Martin went to pick up Bonkers and I stayed home with Molly. I clearly remember Martin walking into the apartment with the dog I never thought I would see again. I'm not sure it was the correct decision for Bonkers, but it was the correct decision for me. I administered his pills and walked him every couple of hours for the next year. Bonkers told us when it was time. He was sleeping in my bathroom and began to shake. Our wonderful vet came to the apartment and gave him a shot. Bonkers immediately relaxed and began to snore a deep, peaceful snore. Martin accompanied Bonkers to the vet for the last time. I couldn't do it.

At the end of my act in Vegas I always asked for questions from the audience. For years one of the questions would always be, "Where's Bonkers?" He was a very special dog.

THE
TWINKLE
YEARS

Kids have so much faith in you. I bought Molly a helium balloon. She let it go in the house. It flew up to the ceiling and she just looked up at me with her big, blue eyes and said, "Mommy, get it." And I got up on a ladder and I got it down for her. Then we went outside. She let it go. It flew up to the universe and she looked up at me with her big, blue eyes, tears streaming down her face, and said, "Mommy, get it." I just couldn't admit to her that there are some things in this world that Mommy can't do for her. So I said, "Ask Daddy to get it."

Twenty

In 2006, the Nevada Ballet named me Las Vegas's Woman of the Year, which was extremely nice of it. A large event was held at the Wynn and my friends Danny Gans and David Brenner kindly agreed to entertain the packed house of ballet supporters, casino executives and celebrities, including Tony Curtis who had recently moved to town. Tony became a friend and to this day we have a painting of his hanging prominently in our house (he was a terrific artist). Every time we met up, Martin pumped him for stories about the golden age of Hollywood, and Tony always obliged, as had Jack Lemmon, Tony's *Some Like It Hot* co-star, years before, when Martin and Jack would chat as they waited for shots to be set up.

The next year, Felix Rappaport left New York-New York and a new president took his place. I think by now you know what's coming. I had averaged 99% business for five years and won Best Comedian at the Best of Las Vegas awards six years in a row, and yet my contract was not renewed. The new guy wanted to try something different. He eventually turned my theater into a nightclub that cost and lost a fortune. It's a Starbucks now.

Felix went to the Luxor, but I chose not to follow him there as I didn't feel the casino's theater was a good fit for me or I for it. Felix understood and we remained firm friends. One night he invited Martin and me to come see Liza Minnelli perform at the Luxor. I love Liza and, even though we were on Broadway during the same time period, our paths had never crossed. Her show at the Luxor was terrific – great dancer, great singer - simply put, Liza is the personification of showbiz. After one particular number, Liza came to the front of the stage and addressed us all.

"Ladies and gentlemen, there's somebody in the audience who's very special to me. She and I are great friends and she's really gotten me through some tough times."

Martin and I looked around, wondering who it could be.

"Please welcome, my dear friend, Rita Rudner."

A spotlight hit me and I stood up, startled. The audience cheered. I waved and blew Liza a kiss. She blew one back.

"I didn't know you knew her," said Martin as I sat down.

"Never met her in my life," I whispered.

In Liza's world, I suspect, reality and fantasy are interchangeable. If in doubt, give 'em the old razzle dazzle. Felix had told her I was in the house and Liza had embroidered a better story. Good for her. I went backstage and we hugged so tightly I almost believed we actually were old friends.

I heard the management at the Venetian was interested in me appearing at their casino. This was ironic; it had been the Venetian's owner, Sheldon Adelson, who imploded his previous property, the Sands, when I had a contract there. Sheldon had built his tribute to Venice on the rubble of the Sands. The casino's president couldn't decide between hiring me or a male impressionist who was new in town. He chose the impressionist.

Luckily, my reputation, and the amount of business I was doing, earned me an offer from another casino and I signed with Harrah's. My head of entertainment at New York-New York, Paula Zappia, had become one of our best friends and it was not an easy move but I have to say (and, yes, I *really* have to say this), I have worked with wonderful people in every Las Vegas hotel I have ever been fortunate enough to perform in. Suzanne Trout was the Harrah's head of entertainment and Laura Ishum was in charge of the day-to-day operations, and what was about to happen to me really depended on their kindness and understanding.

Martin, in the meantime, decided to have an enormous, 30-story-high image of me painted on the side of the Harrah's hotel.

This was another first, although now it's commonplace. Martin's reasoning was twofold: one, it was an extremely effective advertisement, and two, it stared directly into the office of the president of the Venetian right next door. My husband has a vindictive streak!

The Harrah's theater was old-fashioned, but in a good way; cavernous, red-curtained and a little dusty. Although there was theater seating at the front of the house, nearer the back there were red leather booths and drinks were served by waiters and waitresses that had been working in the hotel for decades. Our maître d', Dominic, was an impressive figure. He had been around for all of the illegal shenanigans that had gone on in the years before Vegas became a corporate town. I didn't know the details of Dominic's past, but his present was decidedly kind and caring. After the show, if I didn't have my car at the hotel, Dominic would drive me home and we would listen to Frank Sinatra. I always stopped into his office on my way to the show and we would share dog stories. He knew Bonkers had passed away and his beloved dog had died a few months prior as well. His new love was a poodle puppy he named Mary. Dominic left us recently. He had survived two heart operations, multiple bouts of pneumonia and who knows what else. He was the quintessential tough guy with the big heart. One of my last memories of him was seeing him driving with Mary on his lap, her head happily looking out of the open window, enjoying the breeze.

My show was selling out at Harrah's and Martin had an idea. At the end of my show, I always asked for questions from the audience. Often, one of the questions was, "Do you have any DVDs of your show?" Unfortunately, I didn't own any of my previous specials and when I had contacted HBO to ask why none of them were available, they said they would get back to me. I'm still waiting for that call.

So, Martin thought, "Why not produce our own comedy special?" Since my act is considered squeaky-clean, Martin thought, why not offer it to PBS? The special was called *Rita Rudner: Live From Las Vegas* and was featured on PBS stations across the country. As far as I know, it was and is the only stand-up comedy special that ever aired on PBS.

Our plan was working perfectly. I was able to be a mother and still work, without traveling around the country. Molly was now in kindergarten and already proving to be exceptional in every way. Sorry to sound like every other mother in the universe but of course, in my case, this is true.

At Turnberry Place, the complex within which our apartment was situated, Molly lived like Eloise at the Plaza. She was the only child there. At my request, the builder's developer built a playground just for her. She started playing tennis on the clay courts downstairs when she was barely three, and took lessons from Marty Hennessey, the Turnberry pro and Vegas legend, almost every day. Marty arranged for her to hit with tennis celebrities like the Bryan Brothers, the most successful tennis doubles team of all-time. We'd first met Marty years before at the Desert Inn and enjoyed playing tennis with him and his best friend Tony Bennett, with whom I had then been appearing in the hotel's Starlight Theatre. Marty had two lovely grand-children and Molly would sit with them by Turnberry's magnificent swimming pool, ordering food and drinks and generally having a swell, old time. As Molly's list of school friends grew, that pool became a major hang for a bunch of girls Martin and I secretly referred to as the cast of *The Real Housewives of Las Vegas, 2030*.

Marty, together with a powerhouse named Ryan Wolfington, had recently created a foundation called the Inspiring Children Foundation to help kids attain college scholarships through tennis. The foundation inspires and guides children to be their best selves, and become well-rounded and happy as well as athletically strong. It's been a tremendous success and I consider myself fortunate to have been allowed to become associated with it, however marginally. Molly also benefited from the foundation growing up, making friends with a lot of its participants.

As well as tennis courts and Molly's playground, Turnberry also had a dog park. I had no intention of getting another dog, but Molly had other ideas. Although she never bonded with Bonkers, she was determined to have a dog of her own. She wanted a small dog. One she could pick up. It never occurred to me but Bonkers was 65 pounds. To a small child, he must have looked like an elephant.

About six months after Bonkers left us, Dora, a woman I knew from playing tennis, walked up to me and said, "I know you've lost Bonkers. I run a pet store and have the perfect dog for you." Unfortunately, or fortunately, Molly was with me and heard the conversation.

"Mom, when are we going to see our dog?"

"Sometime."

"When?"

"Sometime."

I remembered how I'd pestered my parents about getting a dog. What goes around comes around, huh? Next day we drove out to Dora's pet store. It was located in a strip mall on the outskirts of Las Vegas and it was different. The dogs were grouped in oversized playpens by breed and a few of them at a time were allowed to run around the store. As we approached, a small dog who looked like a mini-Bonkers put both paws up on the glass door. I was immediately smitten. So was Molly.

"What kind of dog is this?" I asked Dora.

"A Chinese crested powder puff," she explained.

"No, really, what kind of dog is this?"

"Really. You know the dogs with no hair? Sometimes they have hair."

Dora refused to take any money for our new dog. She said, "This is supposed to be your dog."

Dora's pet store no longer exists. Although I'm sure her customers enjoyed taking home free dogs, I'm not sure it was the best business plan.

Molly named our new dog, Twinkle. It took me some time to conjure up deep feelings for a dog again. Although I liked Twinkle immediately, I felt like I was cheating on Bonkers. True to Bonkers' memory, Twinkle never accompanied me to the theater but she gradually worked her way into the special corner of my heart that I save for my dogs.

Meanwhile, every six months or so, Martin, Molly, Twinkle and I would take a few days off to look at beach houses in Laguna. Each time we felt we had saved enough money to buy a house, the prices rose just enough to let us know we hadn't. However, on one trip, the amount of money we had to spend matched a house that we loved. We purchased it that evening.

The house was labeled "soft contemporary." Modern, but not so modern that it looked like you could perform operations in it. The main attribute was an unobstructed view of the Pacific. The vista was so magnificent, I didn't even mind that my hair frizzed.

Twinkle was an extremely energetic puppy. One day, while I was playing ball with her, instead of returning with her ball, she decided to run the other way. The open space of grass had no fence so I ran and grabbed her and fell on the lawn. I didn't think anything of it until later that evening when I tried to take a breath and experienced a sharp pain in my side. I figured it would go away in a few days. It didn't.

Strangely, the pain became more and more pronounced and eventually I couldn't sneeze or yawn because that required too much air. I'm not someone who runs to a doctor every time something goes wrong. I wait and see if things clear up by themselves, but I was having trouble taking in enough air to tell jokes. I would have to breathe in the middle of a punchline. I had to do something.

Martin and I had an exceptional doctor in Las Vegas. I explained my symptoms to him and we began the quest to find out what was going on. First, we tried muscle relaxants. Nope. Then antibiotics. Nope. Then an x-ray where everything appeared normal. Then a urologist. Nope. My gynecologist suggested I stop the hormone replacement pills I had been taking for my hot flashes and the very next day, the pain in my side disappeared and I was able to take deep breaths. What a relief! That's all it was. The stupid hormone pills.

My doctor, however, wasn't satisfied. He strongly suggested my gynecologist perform an internal biopsy. If that sounds painful, that's because it was. I have an annoying habit of singing Christmas carols whenever I have to experience anything unpleasant in a doctor's office. I began singing a beautiful, subtle version of "Jingle Bells" and ended up screaming it in the middle of this particularly barbaric procedure. I had no idea the biopsy would be that excruciating. As I was driving home, I had to pull over into a parking lot and vomit into a bush. I didn't see that coming! I was angry at my doctor for making me go through this unnecessary agony when it was only the stupid hormone pills. I felt fine. When I returned home I immediately put Twinkle on my bed and went to sleep. When I woke up Twinkle was asleep with her head on my shoulder. I think she knew I needed a little extra comforting.

A week later I received a call from my gynecologist. They had received the results from the biopsy and I had uterine cancer. I dropped the phone. Martin picked it up and had the rest of the conversation.

Well, this was just fantastic. I was in the middle of a successful run in Las Vegas and the mother of a five-year-old and I was going to die. Martin immediately went into "we are going to fix this" mode.

"The doctor said you need a hysterectomy and everything will be fine."

"So, that's it? I just need a hysterectomy?"

"Yep."

Dr. Brown recommended a surgeon and off we went to see him and schedule the hysterectomy. We decided to tell nobody except my entertainment directors at Harrah's. I had to take a week off and they had to know why. I was so lucky to have Suzanne Trout and Laura Ishum as my business partners. They were incredibly sympathetic and understanding. They stayed silent and accommodated the dates I requested.

The operation was performed and I was back to work the following week. I was glad that was over! Then we received the phone call about the results. The cancer had been detected in some lymph nodes, so both chemotherapy and radiation were required. What I thought was stage one cancer was really stage three. You never know how you are going to react when you hear that news. The first thing I did was apologize to Martin that I was going to die and leave him to raise our daughter alone. I knew how hard that was, having lived through my mother dying.

I had a talk with my doctor about my treatment. I was sure I would have to quit my job at the casino and just stay home for the next six months. He advised me to do nothing of the kind.

He said, "Wait and see how you respond to the treatment. It's perfectly possible that you will be able to continue working. It's better to keep busy."

My task at hand was to arrange my appearance so as not to alert the public about what was transpiring. Martin went into Martin the producer mode.

"The first thing we're going to do is find a wig you like and then we're going to cut your hair so it is the same as the wig." He then went online and bought me eyebrows, eyelashes and head gear.

I know the phrase "What Happens in Vegas Stays in Vegas" wasn't supposed to apply to cancer, but in my case, it certainly did. At the time of my illness there was a new cancer clinic in Vegas that had been built with the help of Jim Murren, the MGM's CEO, and his wife Heather. I had participated in their charity events. Indeed, the previous year, Stevie Nicks and I had done a fund-raiser for the clinic. Little did I know then that I would be one of its first patients.

Here's one of the drawbacks of any sort of fame. A member of the surgeon's medical staff phoned Norm Clarke, the gossip columnist for the Las Vegas Review Journal, and ratted me out. Norm phoned me to get corroboration and I denied the story. Norm knew me to be a straight arrow so he didn't print the story. Sorry I lied to you, Norm.

The staff at the clinic arranged for me to enter through a side door and get my treatments early so nobody would see me. It is hard enough to make people laugh, but I knew that beginning my act with "So, something funny happened to me in chemo today" was not going to fly.

My doctor was correct. After the first treatment I felt fine and was able to do my show. The steroids that they include in the chemo solution tend to keep you buoyant for the first few days. I began to think what probably crosses very cancer patient's mind: "Maybe my hair won't fall out." I was hoping that would be the case because my new book of essays, *I Still Have it...I Just Can't Remember Where I Put it*, was about to be published. *The View* was filming in Vegas and I was booked to appear on it the following week with Barbara Walters and my two old friends, Whoopi Goldberg and Joy Behar.

The night before I was to film the show, I returned home from the casino and my head began to tingle.

"Martin," I said. "I think my hair is about to fall out."

"Maybe you're just imagining it because you're doing a television show tomorrow," he replied hopefully.

I ran my fingers through my hair and a substantial amount stuck to my hand. Even though you know it's going to happen, and even though you know it will eventually grow back, losing your hair in clumps is a very traumatic experience. Martin helped me pull it out and throw it in the bathroom trash can.

He said, "Who cares what you look like? Who cares about anything? I just want you to be alive."

The next morning, I pulled my wig on and went to Caesars' Palace to appear on *The View*. People told me how much they liked my new haircut.

Molly was six and too young to understand what was going on. I decided to keep the episode from her. The last thing I wanted was for a six-year old to be bombarded with messages that her mother might die. I told her that mommy had to take medicine that was going to make her hair ugly, so I was going to wear a cap at home and a wig when we went outside. That seemed to satisfy her. She is 19 now and I guess I'll have to tell her the truth before she reads this book. The fact that I'm still here 13 years later should lessen the shock.

Martin sat with me for every one of my chemo treatments. I was given the option to do three or four, depending on my tolerance. By the third treatment, my bones were aching and I was constantly nauseous so I stuck at three, knowing that I still had two months of radiation in front of me. My husband, my doctors and my close friends were extremely supportive during this time, but another source of strength was Twinkle. Just her happy presence greeting me whenever I arrived home and her unconditional love picked up my spirits. I never assigned the task of walking her to anyone else. No matter how tired and achy I felt, walking Twinkle always gave me a boost. I learned that trying to maintain a normal way of life was essential for getting through this very abnormal part of my life. Indeed, that would be my advice to anyone faced with a similar bump in the road: continue along the road as best you can. If you pull over to the side, your predicament will become all-consuming and obsessive.

For me, the radiation proved to be even more debilitating than the chemotherapy. Every day I would drop Molly off at school and continue on to the clinic for the treatment. The medical technicians couldn't have been kinder. As I was placed on the machine, they offered me warm blankets and comforting words. However, as you lie in the cylinder and are alone with your thoughts, you can't help but contemplate the curve ball that has been thrown at you. I tried to stay positive but as I exited the machine for the first time, the only positive thought I could conjure was, "Only 39 treatments to go. How am I ever going to do this?"

I did, and by the end of the second month I had every side effect that doctors had warned me about. I don't want to go into great detail, but there were times when I was on stage at the casino that I thought I might have to excuse myself and come back a little later. Only my closest friends were aware of my circumstances. My day-to-day acquaintances were totally unaware of my situation. People would say, "You lost weight and I love your hair! You look terrific!"

"Thank you," I would reply, thinking, "If you only knew."

I looked up the weather in Honolulu before we went there. It said, "Sunny with a chance of lava."

Twenty-one

I was asked by Nevada's senator and at that time democratic leader of the Senate Harry Reid to perform at a democratic fundraiser at Caesars' Palace that would feature our new president Barack Obama, Sheryl Crow and Bette Midler. Harry wanted me to emcee the event. I have never included any political material in my act. I vote and I take part in fundraisers for candidates I believe in, but I don't like to preach when people pay to come and see me. I certainly have my own beliefs, rooted in the desire for this country to pursue social equality and equal opportunity for all, and I'm happy to debate anyone at any time on any issue, except when I'm on stage. That's not what I'm selling. Given that, this invitation by Harry Reid was certainly a challenging event for a non-political comedian, but I seldom decline a challenge. I also had an ulterior motive; I wanted Molly to meet the president.

The event was located in the Caesars' Palace Colosseum which seats over 4,000 people. The room had been built for Celine Dion, whom I joked had copied me by committing to a Las Vegas residency. On a serious note, I don't think it's a coincidence that so many women ended up in residency in Las Vegas – Celine, Bette Midler, Cher, Britney Spears, Mariah Carey, Shania Twain, Jennifer Lopez (wonder if she remembers me?!), Lady Gaga and Katy Perry. It's certainly a long way from when the Sands refused to let me appear without a male co-headliner. Today's Las Vegas treats everything as a win/lose proposition – you either sell tickets or you don't. There's a purity and fairness to that, and it negates the sexism that undoubtedly exists in other aspects of show business.

Martin and I collaborated on writing some topical jokes. I can't remember any of them now and even if I did remember them, they wouldn't make any sense at this point in our political landscape. That's another reason I don't include politics in my act. It changes too quickly. I leave it to comedians who have a nightly show and writers that can keep up with the daily news. I like to write jokes about human behavior because the truisms contained in those jokes tend to have a long, multi-generational shelf-life.

The day of the show, Martin, Molly and I were escorted back to our dressing room by Secret Service agents. Security was understandably intense – snipers on the roof, bomb-sniffing dogs, constant searches, perimeter guards, and no doubt lots of stuff I wasn't aware of. I nervously went over my portion of the show until an agent came to deliver us to the official meeting place. Molly and I were escorted to the room to wait for the president and Senator Reid with Sheryl and Bette.

When they arrived, President Obama immediately began telling Molly about the playground they had just built for his daughters out of recycled tires at the White House. He even told her she could come play with Sasha and Malia. Many photos were taken.

"When are we going to Washington for my play date?" Molly asked as I tucked her into bed that night.

"He's very nice, but he's still a politician," I told her. "I wouldn't hold your breath."

As I type this in our office, behind me is a photo of a seven-year-old Molly standing in front of Bette Midler and Sheryl Crow, shaking Barack Obama's hand. I'm in the photo too, wearing the wig that everyone liked better than my real hair, even though it was beginning to look a little wiggy.

Molly's favorite TV show was *Hannah Montana*. She and Martin watched every episode together from the pilot onwards. When Miley Cyrus came to town to appear as Hannah Montana at the MGM, I quickly reserved tickets. Molly had been taking piano lessons and, unlike her mother, had shown an enormous aptitude for it. They day after seeing Miley and meeting her backstage (hey, I have Vegas juice), Molly begged us for a guitar. We were only too happy to grant her request. Who knew that only a few years later, she'd be good enough to start appearing sometimes as my opening act.

My run at Harrah's lasted three years and then my contract was over and a new entertainment director arrived. Suzanne and Laura both departed. Rita went too. However, the painting of me on the side of the building must have had an effect. After staring at it for three years, and the impressionist having not worked out, the Venetian president made me an offer I couldn't refuse.

It was a reduced schedule of three days a week with no shows in the summer, and at that point in my life, that suited me just fine. In fact, a year or so later, I ended up cutting that schedule down even further as Joan Rivers, David Spade and Tim Allen agreed to share the space with me. My hair was coming back, but my energy level was taking a little longer. I don't know if this has happened to other chemotherapy patients, but my hair came back fried. It was as though I had been electrocuted from the inside, which in a way is exactly what happened. I hadn't been outside without my wig for nine months and my head was becoming itchy.

I got an offer to do two concerts in Maui. Summer was coming in Las Vegas and Molly had just graduated from the first grade, so I took some time off before beginning at the Venetian and Martin, Molly and I flew off to Hawaii. Outside of Las Vegas nobody recognized me and I sat by the pool with my ugly, real hair poking out of my scalp. It felt so liberating.

I still wore my wig on stage. The Maui theater was far away from the hotel and attracted locals, not tourists, so I figured that nobody in the hotel would ever be at my show. The day after the show, I was walking around the hotel with my fried hair and a person who had been at my show spotted me. She pointed at my head and laughed. I heard her say to her friend, "Look, Rita Rudner is wearing a silly wig." I ran back to my room before she was able to get any closer.

Other than that, our Hawaii vacation was a welcome change of scene. Molly fell in love with Hawaii and still thinks she may live there one day. One of the features of the hotel was a package that offered swimming with dolphins. I've always admired dolphins from afar and that was the way I would have preferred to keep it. However, that darn Las Vegas school had taught Molly to read and so she pointed out to me, while holding the brochure, that we could be swimming with dolphins right downstairs. There was no way Martin was going to jump into what he so eloquently described as a "fish toilet." I was elected to fulfill Molly's dream.

Dolphins must have very good managerial representatives because they charge quite a bit to let you near them. I remember it being around $300 and, if you want to take photos, add another $100 onto their fee. D-Day came and I thought I'd gotten lucky. It was raining.

I called down and asked, "Do you still have your dolphin program active when it's raining?"

"Yes," the dolphin's manager said. "The dolphins don't care. They're already wet."

Molly and I wandered down to dolphin headquarters in the storm and donned our dolphin gear. As I slid down into the slimy pool, I wondered if this would make Molly love me more when she grew up or if she would forget all about it. I decided to buy the photograph package and hang the pictures on her bedroom wall to accrue future maternal brownie points.

We swam alongside the dolphins, fed the dolphins, petted the dolphins and ended up, in our final photograph, kissing a particularly affectionate dolphin. The slime factor in the water was definitely unpleasant. The good thing about the experience was that it didn't ruin my hair; the bad thing was that I never felt the same about that bathing suit.

It took another full year for my hair to calm down and come to its senses. Again, I continued my lucky streak of working with people who were terrific. Al was my house manager at the Venetian and he and I always shared stories about our beloved dogs. My reduced schedule gave me more home time with my family and gradually the trauma of my ill health and treatment began to fade into the distance.

Martin had been writing a movie script and researching state-of-the-art cameras that were being employed by some new semi-reality shows like MTV's *Laguna Beach*. The new cameras were making video look like film. Film is time-consuming and expensive. Video, however, is quick and cheap. Martin decided that the following summer we would film a movie in our beach house.

I had very little to do with the project until it was up and running. Martin wrote the script, directed it, budgeted it, hired the entire crew, and arranged accommodations. You name it, he did it. We used the talented actors we had worked with previously at New York-New York in *BOO!*, as well as veteran actor Paul Dooley, whose work we had always admired. I provided the cast with outfits and costume jewelry.

The entire shoot lasted ten days. The only room in our house that wasn't used for the movie was my bathroom. I always had a scented candle burning and nicknamed the space "The bathroom of tranquility." I was also available to freshen the actors' hair and make-up. Our neighbors were generous and allowed us to use their garage for lunches and dinners because our garage was full of lighting equipment. Some of the scenes were filmed on the beach and one scene was filmed on a friend's yacht.

The movie is called *Thanks*. It charts the changes in a family over three Thanksgivings. I cooked three turkeys plus the side dishes for the multiple holiday feasts. I also washed a lot of dishes. Once it was completed, we sent it to a few nearby film festivals for potential inclusion. Much to our delight, the prestigious Palm Springs Film

Festival decided to premiere it. The Palm Springs Film Festival happens in January, just prior to the Golden Globes, and kicks off awards season. Our little film was going to rub celluloid (actually, videotape, but you get the idea) with film stars and big-time directors. Martin and I invited the cast and crew who'd been involved in the film to Palm Springs and to participate in a Q&A with the audience after its screening. We drank a lot of champagne, had our photos taken on the red carpet and did a lot of laughing.

Thanks went on to win awards at several different film festivals and was eventually sold to Showtime. I know it wasn't a big Hollywood movie that grossed a zillion dollars, but there is something to be said for being your own boss and doing something the way you want to do it. I'm very proud of this film, and even prouder of my hair in this film. Maybe check it out on the internet? We think it's our best movie. It's also probably our last movie. Martin and I, as you may have noticed, like the immediacy of live performance. There's too much hanging around for me with film and TV work. Do show. Get check. Go home. That's my favorite showbiz recipe. However, psychically *Thanks* was a great palate cleanser for us and, with Molly playing in the waves in its beginning montage and the house we would eventually sell as its main location, for me it's an emotionally satisfying testimony to that period of our lives.

A few months after our Palm Springs Film Festival adventure, I was told somebody wanted to pay me to fly to Singapore to perform at a birthday party. Not just any party: Sheldon Adelson's 80th birthday party. Sheldon Adelson, as previously noted, was the billionaire owner of the Venetian. I had performed at his wife, Miriam's birthday party a few months earlier, but that was in the hotel where I worked, and a lot easier to get to.

There was another problem. The day after the party in Singapore, I was booked in New Jersey. I was well within the limits of my contract, which gave me a 60-day cancellation clause, but the New Jersey booker, Neil, was distraught.

"It's sold out. Everybody is looking forward to it!" he justifiably moaned.

"She'll re-schedule. I promise," my agent Steve replied.

"My reputation as a promoter is at stake. You can't do this to me."

Steve called Martin.

"What do you want to do? She'd make a lot more money in Singapore, but Neil is suicidal."

Martin put on his thinking cap.

"There has to be a way she can do both."

You'll recall we'd had a similar problem years before on New Year's Eve in Las Vegas when I had been offered two great gigs on the same night. Martin figured out that Singapore was a day ahead of New Jersey. If I left immediately after Sheldon's party, I would gain a day on the way back. I could literally do two shows on the same day, so long as one was in Singapore and the other was in New Jersey. There was a flight out of Singapore at 1:00 a.m. It connected through Hong Kong. It would arrive in New Jersey at 2:00 in the afternoon and I would have plenty of time before the show at 7:00. I might be slightly woozy, but everyone would be happy. I accepted both gigs.

I'd never flown first class in one of those fancy planes where you actually have a real bed. I can heartily recommend it if someone else is paying for it. The food was scrumptious, I watched two movies and slept better than a baby. (I never understood the expression "slept like a baby." My baby kept waking up and demanding food.)

I was met in Singapore by Sheldon's people and driven to his hotel, the Marina Bay Sands, which is one of the most spectacular buildings in the world. I arrived at the VIP check in at around 10:00 in the morning and was met there by Chan, my butler, who escorted me to my suite. The one-bedroom suite was decorated in the style of a sleek Manhattan apartment. On one side were city views which were impressive, but the view from the enormous bathroom was what I remember the most. Mingling in the Singapore Strait were all different types of colorful fishing boats. The free-standing bathtub was directly in front of the picture window overlooking the Strait. For the first hour I was there, I just sat in the bathtub and watched the fishing show.

The pool on the roof of the Marina Bay Sands is an architectural marvel: an infinity pool that joins the three towers of the hotel together. It appears as if you could just swim to the end of the roof and fall over into the abyss. Many of the hotel guests lounged around the pool and watched their children swim to the edge. I got a little worried but all of the parents happily sipped their drinks and, as far as I know, all of the children survived.

Sometimes the timing is right for strange things to happen. One of my friends, Lisa, happened to be in Singapore, choreographing for the Singapore Ballet. We had lived in the same building in New York when she was a ballerina with the New York City Ballet and I was becoming a comedian. She and her sister Bonnie (also a phenomenal ballerina with NYCB) and I had been firm friends for decades.

Lisa and I met for dinner. We couldn't believe that we were getting together to have dinner in a glamorous hotel in Singapore. We planned to meet on the moon in 2030. The menu in the chic restaurant featured many items we were unfamiliar with. Lisa and I avoided the more graphic offerings of fried chicken feet and fermented eggs and stuck with the sautéed veggies and fried rice. I felt other patrons watch our food arrive and look down on us.

The next day was devoted to organizing my act for the party. Performing at private functions is much more difficult than performing in a theater or club. The material has to be specific to the audience in order to hold their attention. They certainly didn't come to Sheldon's birthday party to see me! Early in the day, I received a call from Paul Anka who was performing the following evening for Sheldon and his friends. It was evidently a multi-day celebration. I had met Paul a few times before.

"Hi Rita. I understand you're doing your act for the party tonight."

"Yes. You are correct. How can I help you?"

"What are you going to talk about?" he inquired.

"Funny you should ask. I'm putting together my set right now."

"I just want to make sure you're not going to talk about birthday parties because I'm going to do stuff on that."

"Oh," I replied. "I'm so glad you're going to tell jokes, because I was planning to sing 'My Way.'"

"No, really, I don't think we should step on each other's material."

A few years before, I would have said, "What don't you want me to talk about and I'll try not to mention those things?" but now I just said, "I think you're going to have to risk it. Have a wonderful time tomorrow night." That was the end of the conversation.

I went downstairs at about 3:00 to check the sound, lights and room. The area was decorated entirely in white; tablecloths, chairs, flowers and curtains, all bright white. It looked like a giant bag of flour on the ceiling had exploded. I made a mental note not to mention that. The room wasn't large; there were maybe 20 circular tables, each seating eight. Circular tables are bad news for comedians. Half of the people are facing the wrong way and, for some reason, they don't want to turn their chairs. People would rather face the table and try to alter their heads. Here's another thing you would have no reason to know: the smaller the group, the harder it is to make people laugh. If you are performing to a thousand people, the odds of someone finding you funny greatly increase.

I went back to my room and decided to end my act with a personalized poem. I had done some research on Sheldon's past and found out that he had begun his career selling newspapers on a corner in Boston and had later become a taxi driver. Sheldon was truly a self-made man. Keep in mind this was well before he became a huge Trump donor, so I didn't have to include anything political, which is a good thing because I don't think he would have enjoyed what I had to say.

As well as preparing for the show, I had to pack my suitcase. I was off-stage at 8:30 and my flight back to New Jersey was at 10:00. The show went as well as could be expected. I told the story about my first big Las Vegas contract at the Sands and how Sheldon blew up the hotel before it began. I talked about marriage and children and yes, birthdays (sorry, Paul) and ended with my poem. Then I was off to the airport and arrived in plenty of time. The only problem was that the incoming plane was late. There was an inconvenient typhoon in Hong Kong, which was where my connection to New Jersey was taking place. I was still in Sheldon's Singapore, so I waited in the VIP lounge. A chicly-dressed woman informed me at about 11:00 p.m. that the plane was being delayed for the foreseeable future and offered me a back room with a bed and blanket.

"We will wake you up when we have more information," she purred.

"I have a connection in Hong Kong! I have to get to New Jersey. Will I be able to do that?"

"There are no flights going in or out of Hong Kong at this time. I will wake you if I have more information."

Martin's plan had definitely hit a snag. I re-located to a back room and tried to go to sleep at around midnight, but I couldn't. How was I going to trust that someone would remember to wake me up? I tried closing my eyes for a few minutes and imagined the plane leaving without me. My eyes remained open until 2:00 a.m. when a different but equally chicly-dressed woman came in and said, "Your plane is now boarding."

An airport cart whisked me to the plane. I could get used to this VIP treatment! When the plane landed in Hong Kong, I assumed I would have ample time to catch my next flight, since all the planes had been delayed. That was not the case. I had less than half an hour before my flight to New Jersey left. I looked around for the VIP treatment. It wasn't there. I was no longer in Sheldon's Singapore. I was in Rita's Hong Kong. The gate was on the other side of the airport. I tried to hail an airport cart. It cost money and I didn't have Hong Kong currency. I ran with my suitcase and was stopped at customs.

"I have to get to my flight," I complained.

"You have to get in line," the customs officer insisted.

"I know Sheldon!" I said.

Nothing.

It took 15 minutes to get through customs. I had five minutes to find my plane. I arrived as the doors were closing and took my seat. I was on my way to New Jersey. Neil wouldn't get fired. Martin's plan was back on track. I ordered a mimosa.

We took a cruise this year because friends of ours took a cruise and had a great time. It depends on the boat. You have to get on a good boat. They've got the Fantasy and the Ecstasy. We were on the Hysterectomy.

Twenty-two

People always ask me if I get bored telling the same jokes every night. I don't, because every single night I go on stage, I try something new. Of course, most of my act is pre-planned. I would never expect an audience to sit through an hour and a half of untested material, but if I don't at least try to include a new idea every time I go on stage, I consider the evening a failure, even if the audience does not. The repetition of performing a nightly show in Las Vegas helped me develop the skill of being relaxed on stage while maintaining focus and concentration. I think that is the ultimate goal of every performer and athlete.

Speaking of athletes, Molly had become an avid tennis player. Martin and I spent a lot of time driving to tennis tournaments and trying to keep our tempers. We were not ideal tennis parents. Coaching is illegal during tournaments and Martin had to walk away a number of times during matches, unable to control his controlling instincts. I felt Molly wasn't practicing enough and I took the game way too seriously. She won many tournaments but ultimately, if tennis is not something you want to use to obtain a college scholarship or try to turn professional, it's better to play for fun. Molly wasn't having any, and eventually she turned her attention full-time towards music.

I have to fight against my tiger mom instincts constantly. As you now know, when I was growing up, all I wanted to do was dance. I spent every night at ballet class and every weekend rehearsing classical ballets. I loved it. It made me happy to be the best I could be at one thing. I've come to realize that my home life was so unpleasant, I had to escape. Molly is a much more balanced child than I ever was. But has she practiced piano today???? Has she played her new song on the guitar???? There I go again. Stop it, Rita.

For years I'd been offered jobs on cruise ships, but hadn't wanted to take the time off from my Las Vegas schedule. Now, my summers were up for grabs. We visited places I'd always wanted to go (Venice, St. Tropez, Monte Carlo, Barcelona, the Bahamas) as well as places I didn't know existed (Bora Bora, Tonga, Elba). Molly has always been up for adventure and because Martin is the opposite, I've found myself in unexpected places. Of all the positions I've been in, I think zip-lining down a mountain in New Zealand has to have been my least favorite. Why is that fun? I have no idea. Helmeted, straight-jacketed and practically sewn into a seat while sliding down a clothes line is not my idea of a good time. However, Molly loved it and I loved that she loved it. She loved it so much she made me record her hurling down the zip-line while I was hurling down the zip-line parallel to her so she could post the video on social media.

As with my material on-stage, I'm always up for trying something new, especially if suggested by Molly. Snorkeling with stingrays, swimming with lemon sharks, whitewater rafting, water slides – I've done them all with good grace while Martin sat comfortably in a nearby bar, smirking. He did join me for one adventure. We took Molly and her friend on a mountain hike to three waterfalls in Hawaii. About five minutes into the hike, our guide found two sticks and handed them to Martin and me to use as canes. It rained the night before so the ground was extremely muddy. Those sneakers never made the trip back to my closet. Martin and I slowly made our way to the first two waterfalls, but bailed on the third one when we saw the vertical climb ahead of us. We waited on the rocks below and let the guide take Molly and her friend up the slippery mountain, praying that we would see them again. When they made it back down the hill, even they said it was a little scary. You probably think I'm exaggerating the danger aspect of this trip, but as we exited the woods there were two men carrying a broken-legged woman into the back of an ambulance. As I was leaving, I spotted a woman embarking on the treacherous journey with her two children. I wished her luck and gave her my cane.

My most recent brush with danger came in Alaska. The cruise was relaxing and the scenery was amazing. Molly, however, wanted to take a helicopter trip and climb a glacier. The morning of our trip, I had a ray of hope. Fog was settling in and if I looked hard enough the fog was spelling cancellation. But wait, the fog cleared and we were on our way.

I've been on planes my whole life. However, I'm used to runways, not lift-offs. Helicopters leap up into the sky with no warning. Molly was seated next to me, enjoying the expansive view. I was clutching onto her leg like a tick. The helicopter landed on the ice and, as the wind whipped around us, we struggled for our balance on the frozen surface. Yes, it was pretty, but I've never been so cold. Nothing can really prepare you for standing on a windy glacier. And nothing should. There is really no reason to do it unless you want your daughter to have a good time. Our guide smeared mud on our faces and said it was good for our skin. I think he was just making fun of us. Molly bent down on the ice to drink from a frozen stream. She said it was delicious. I took her word for it.

I consider these moments that I shared with my daughter invaluable. How lucky am I to be dragged, out of my comfort zone and experience feelings I could never imagine with a human being that I love more than anybody on earth? When I told my father that Martin and I were going to adopt a child, he said, "It's a big risk. You have a good career and a good marriage; it's like you have a perfectly set table and you're knocking it over." We knocked it over and we're so glad we did!

Speaking of knocking things over, Martin had always wanted to build a house from scratch. We loved our beach house, but there were elements about it we wanted to change. We looked at properties for a few months and decided to stay where we were and not knock over our perfectly set table. Until - one day, Martin found a house whose price had been reduced four times. We were taking a walk on the beach and Martin looked up at a house on a hill and said, "I think that's the house with the price-cuts. We have to go and see it."

We called our realtor and she said, "It's in escrow, but I'll call and see if I can show it to you anyway."

The next day, we met her at the house. I immediately realized why it was reduced. "Eclectic" does not begin to tell the story. It was Japanese meets South-western with African influences. It also smelled of wet moldy hay and cat urine. My eyes watered and I had to wait outside. Martin braved the tour. He said when he emerged, "You smell cat pee. You know what I smell?" "What?" I asked. "Opportunity."

The offer in escrow fell through and we made a proposal that was accepted. We were the proud owners of a smelly tear-down with a teppanyaki bar in the middle of the living room. Its curb appeal was minimal - it consisted of a huge square structure interrupted by an aging brown garage door. We nicknamed the house "the Toaster."

The process of tearing a house down and getting plans drawn up and approved takes a long time, especially in a coastal community with ocean issues, so we decided to rent out our strange house for the summer months while we stayed in Las Vegas. First, Martin, Molly and I went to work on the cleaning process. I scrubbed the walls, we painted, bought new beds and bedding, sofa covers, cleaned the carpets and rented that sucker out. It turned out to be the perfect rental because we really didn't care if anyone broke or spilled anything. Even setting it on fire would be a good thing.

I'd heard nightmare stories about couples building houses together. The consensus was that the process usually ended in either divorce or bankruptcy. Cutting to the end, we're still married and we aren't destitute, but I won't deny the process was a little stressful. A year was spent arguing about where the natural hill in front of our house legally ended and where our property began. We fought with the city, the coastal commission, our soils inspector and our homeowners' association. The coastal commission wanted the pool to start so far back on our property there would be no room for the house. The soil was too sandy for a certain type of foundation and Martin had to find a waiver in the city library from 1972 that allowed us to build to the height of the house we were tearing down.

When you're planning to build a house from scratch you have to make decisions on items you never knew existed.

"Do you want a museum edge on your wall or a skirting board?" our chic designer Melissa asked me.

"Well, I don't want my wall to wear a skirt, but I also don't want to live in a museum," I replied. "What are my other choices?"

Melissa recommended a museum edge and we agreed with her, even though we had no idea what she was talking about. She was so stylish, we figured she was correct. Melissa was impossibly thin and beautifully dressed 100% of the time. She showed up wearing stilettos to building sites and managed to keep her balance in incredibly un-even situations.

Meanwhile, Martin and I attended every open house in our area and took pictures of design ideas that we might incorporate into our new adventure. I have very little decorating ability, so any time I can actually see something that someone else has done that works, I get excited. I don't think stealing a window treatment idea is illegal. At least, I hope not, otherwise I am going to designer jail.

Two years after purchasing the property, we were ready to begin. As we stood in the middle of the street and watched a wrecking ball barrel through the Toaster, Martin said, "I've got to stop having ideas."

Martin is excited to go back to England. He's looking forward to seeing some of his old friends. Especially the ones that have less hair than he does.

Twenty-three

With construction at the new house in California progressing slowly but inexorably, and the weather turning toasty in Las Vegas, I accepted a summer cruise offer. The ship left from Barcelona, which meant we could first visit old friends in London. I was also offered a small fee to appear at an event called the *Latitude Festival*.

We planned to stay in London for two weeks and we thought it might be more fun to rent an apartment than stay in a hotel. Martin corresponded with a man who had a flat in a part of North London that was close to many of our friends. We looked at the photos of the apartment online. It looked cute.

Meanwhile, we had previously relied on a couple who lived in our Las Vegas building and were Twinkle's alternate parents whenever we were out of town. However, they had recently moved. How inconsiderate can you get?! I collected recommendations and interviewed possible replacements. Twinkle's groomer recommended a woman who lived nearby and I stopped in to visit to make sure she was a true dog lover. Lynda passed the test. She had turned her apartment into one big dog bed. There were pillows and blankets everywhere and I spotted three dogs relaxing in various states of Zen. I noticed a sound in the room.

"What's that?" I inquired.

"It's my sound machine. I keep it on the ocean noise. That seems to be the dogs' favorite."

The three of us arrived at the given address in London. We stood on the sidewalk alongside our four oversized, overweight suitcases plus Molly's guitar and rang the bell. Nothing. We rang it again and a very pleasant, middle-aged Englishman appeared.

"You must be the Bergmans. Welcome," he said. "Sorry, I was just cleaning the apartment upstairs."

"Upstairs?" Martin asked, looking up at a series of stairs.

"Yes, I converted my attic into an apartment. It's only a few flights up."

It took a couple of trips and a multitude of grunts, but our host was helpful in pushing the suitcases from behind while we pulled. The tiny apartment had tiny charm. Since it was an attic, the ceilings were sloped and the skylights made it easy to see the rain. The closet-sized kitchen possessed a coffee maker, mini-fridge and a narrow table that resembled half of an ironing board. Our host disappeared down the stairs quickly. I think I heard him say, "Call if you don't need anything."

Molly lucked out by staying in the living room, which was the largest room in the apartment. She had her own television, which she does not have at home, so she was beyond thrilled. The only problem with her room was that her bed was under the skylights and the skylights didn't fully close and, being London, it rained three or four times a day. We used her raincoat as a blanket.

Martin and I had a small, dark bedroom that proved to be somewhat home-made. Martin hung two suits up in the cubby hole sized closet and the rack fell to the floor. He tried to re-fasten it. He didn't want to tell our host that we had broken his closet, so he never hung anything up again. Martin sat on the bed and leaned back to rest but his side of the bed gave way. He tumbled down the slant to the floor. It was less a bed than it was a ride. We tried to shore it back up, not wanting to tell our host we had broken his bed as well as the closet.

After getting acquainted with our attic's idiosyncrasies, we had a wonderful time. The three of us not being able to fit in the kitchen at the same time proved to be a blessing. We found a trendy coffee shop a block away and enjoyed cappuccinos and pastries together every morning. Martin's birthday was a few days away and Molly and I bought him a certificate at a local spa for a "Four Handed Massage." I wasn't sure if it was one person with four hands, one person with two real hands and two fake hands or two people with two hands each, but it certainly sounded birthday-worthy.

We had dinner with friends, did some sight-seeing and bought lots of umbrellas that broke.

Then it was time to visit the *Latitude Festival*. No one was really able to describe the event to me. The closest they came was, "Woodstock, but not really." The festival was unreachable by train or plane, so we hired a car and a driver.

The next day, about three hours into our journey I asked the driver if we were almost there.

He answered with a brief, "No."

The next two hours were a series of winding roads that made all of us queasy. The last road proved to be rather muddy and our wheels began to spin. I spotted a pair of wooden gates ahead and a young man came running towards us.

"This has been happening a bit today. Rained again last night, and this morning and this afternoon."

He positioned himself at the back of the car as our driver put his foot on the accelerator. As we lurched forward out of the ditch with the help of our kindly pusher, our driver exclaimed, "We're here."

Peter, our pusher, led us to a trailer.

"This is all yours," he said. "You're welcome to wait here or wander about the festival."

"When am I on?"

"Let's see, it's 2:00 now. I'll come get you around 5:00."

"But you told me to be here by 2:00."

"We like to know people are here. Some of the performers turn back."

The three of us decided to explore the *Latitude Festival*. It was kind of like Woodstock, but with sheep. I called it Sheepstock.

There were various menus written on blackboards in front of food trucks, Blood pudding, spotted dick, scones with clotted cream. You know….health food. Tents had been set up for musical acts and, as I mentioned, there were sheep. And mud. Mucho mud.

I took some notes to see if I could incorporate any local jokes in my act. Let's see, I'm in a muddy field in the middle of nowhere, my hair is frizz central, my feet are freezing, I'm hungry and the only thing I can find to eat has either blood, dick or clot in the title. Was that funny? Or was it just true?

We went back to my warm trailer and waited to be called for my show. My trailer contained a small package of M&Ms and a can of Coke, which I donated to Molly and Martin for their dinner.

I was escorted to my performing tent by a sheep. Only kidding. It was a cordial young man who looked a little like a sheep. We squished our way to the tent where I would be performing and I stood on the side, listening to the comedian that I would follow.

There is no gentle way to describe his act. He was recreating a camping trip. He was looking for a place to go to the bathroom. He found a pot. In the last ten minutes of his act, he graphically described how he accomplished the difficult task of, as he put it, "shitting in a pot." After he thoroughly described the act, I think he actually produced a pot and acted it out. It's not that his act wasn't funny. It was very funny. The audience enjoyed it. It's just that my act is subtle. Remember the Chevy Chase roast? A clean act has difficulty following a dirty act. It doesn't matter how funny the clean act is, the punch of swear words dulls the tickle of imagery.

As Mr. Pot was finishing, I heard strange noises coming from the tent next door. First a few electric guitar riffs, then a piano and then some drums.

"What's that?" I asked the sound technician.

"That's the band in the tent next door. They're really good."

"And what time do they start?" I asked.

"Five."

I was introduced and walked on stage to thunderous music and applause. Unfortunately, the music and applause were coming from the tent to the right of me.

I've never done this before or since, but I cut my time short. I was supposed to do 40 minutes and I could only manage 20. I just told the audience, I wasn't going to bother doing set ups because nobody could hear me anyway. I was just going to do punchlines. And that's what I did. Then I told the audience to go and see the band playing in the tent next door. I'd heard they were really good.

I told the organizer he didn't have to pay me, but he insisted. I was glad he insisted and didn't put up much of a fight. I bought a cup that says *Latitude Festival* on it. I want to remember I was there so I never go back again.

We spent three more days in our London attic and then packed up to fly to Barcelona. Hauling our suitcases down the flights of stairs was a bit easier than pulling them up, but I still wouldn't recommend it. I would however, recommend Barcelona. Every corner contains something magical. The outdoor markets, churches, shops, buildings and museums are all breathtakingly wonderful. We stayed in a fabulous hotel that had a spectacular restaurant located on its roof. This restaurant overlooked ornate, mad Gaudi architecture that is the hallmark of Barcelona. It served imaginative, creative, delicious tapas plus the best sangria, served in a balloon-shaped glass filled with oranges and lemons and a mixture of juices and red wines that I have never been able to recreate. Inevitably, after a long day of sightseeing, I would say to Martin, "We can't eat at the hotel restaurant again!" Martin would say, "I know!" And we would end up eating in the hotel restaurant, admiring La Sagrada Familia as we sipped on sangria.

After three days in Barcelona, we were ready to board the ship for our next adventure. We celebrated Molly's 14th birthday that evening in the floating dining room. I felt extremely fortunate to be able to vacation with my family and get paid at the same time. On an eight-day cruise, I was asked to perform on only two nights to a packed, receptive audience. The rest of the time was spent eating, drinking and deciding what off-shore excursions might be acceptable to both Martin and Molly. Cruising in the Mediterranean didn't provide many death-defying acts, so Martin and I were able to persuade Molly to attend a lunch in Portofino.

"What are they going to have to eat?" she asked.

"Delicious food."

"Pizza?"

"Of course," I replied, not knowing if they would have pizza.

The next day, a group of us boarded a bus and traveled up a narrow, winding road to one of the most elegant hotels I have ever seen, and I have seen some nice digs!

It was called Hotel Splendido and splendido, it was. Nestled in a verdant mountainside, the hotel overlooked Portofino Harbor and offered a view of the mega yachts resting in the Mediterranean below. There was an infinity edged pool overlooking the sea and impossibly-thin, tan, bikini-clad women were reclining in lounge chairs, sipping exotic drinks. Even 14-year-old Molly was impressed.

"Someday, I'm going to live here!" she declared.

"Okay. I'll be visiting you frequently if you can pull that off."

"How much will it cost?" Molly asked.

"Let's get a brochure and see."

We found the front desk and perused a pamphlet.

"Do you want to live in a single room or a suite?"

"A suite."

"Okay. Off season, it's $3,000 a night."

"Maybe I'll just come here again for lunch."

"Good thinking."

I hate killing young people's dreams, but sometimes you just have to.

At 1:00 we gathered in the restaurant overlooking the impossibly turquoise water. Our guide announced that, before lunch, we would be sampling different kinds of olive oil.

"What??" Molly whispered. "What am I tasting?"

"Olive oil. Don't worry, we are dipping bread in it. You like bread."

Our guide passed around tiny paper cups filled with our first offering.

"I think you'll find this olive oil a bit fruity but with a hint of sarcasm that really can't be explained."

We all dipped our bread in the tiny paper cups and tasted our witty oil. We all agreed that this was a fruity, insouciant oil. Another tiny paper cup was passed around.

"This oil comes from an olive farm at the top of a hill. It has a strong, insistent tone of voice. I think you'll taste its ruggedness and determination."

Again, we dipped and agreed.

Molly asked, "Mom, when do we get the pizza?"

"One more pretentious oil to go and, oh yes, I lied about the pizza."

Our last oil was delicate and had been to the ballet.

Molly might have complained but, as a result of this lunch, she never butters her bread and always asks for olive oil when we eat in a restaurant. She also has opinions concerning its tone of voice.

Pasta pesto was served for lunch and it was so extraordinarily good, Molly forgot about the pizza.

After lunch, Molly, Martin and I found a flower-covered gazebo and tried to hide so we wouldn't have to leave.

The next port of call after Portofino was Marseille, which I'm reliably informed is in France. Martin had always wanted to visit a nearby town called Aix. We hopped in a cab and said, "Please take us to Aix."

In 20 minutes, we arrived at a vibrant street fair in picturesque and quintessentially French Aix. Our friendly cab driver said he would return to drive us back to the ship in a couple of hours. What a nice guy, I thought. Martin, Molly and I wandered around the various stalls and bought a few French items. I don't want to imply that I'm a boring person but I found some fabulous dish towels that I still cherish.

Our taxi driver duly appeared at the designated time and area to drive us back to the Marseilles docks. The mistake was made when Martin sat me next to the driver.

"Are you sure you want to go back to the ship?" he asked, in his beautiful French accent.

"Why?" I answered. "Where else should we go?"

Our driver, who I will call "Mani" (short for manipulator) pulled out an iPad.

"Look at this!"

I looked. I saw fields of lavender. The hypnotic, violet fields penetrated my retinas and forced themselves into my brain. I obeyed my impulse and foolishly asked, "How far are they?"

Mani replied, "10 minutes."

I turned around to Martin and Molly who were sitting innocently in the back seat.

"I've always wanted to see the lavender fields. When else are we going to be here? They're not far."

"Okay," Martin answered. "As long as they're not too far."

"Dix minutes." Mani repeated.

Forty minutes later, I desperately asked Mani, "How much longer?"

"Dix minutes." Mani replied.

I heard Molly whisper to Martin, "I think we've been kidnapped."

"We can't turn back now. We're almost there," I pleaded. "I've always wanted to see the lavender."

"It is only ten minutes more." Mani explained. Then, sensing Martin's anger radiating from the back seat, Mani again picked up his iPad with his non-driving hand and showed me a picture of a sunflower field.

"It's a sunflower field," I explained, stating the obvious. "I've always wanted to see the sunflower fields."

"10 minutes," stated Mani.

After 20 minutes we turned onto a dirt road and there they were. Fields of lavender. We exited the taxi and as I wandered into the lavender, I noticed that bees also like lavender. Molly, who is sensibly afraid of bees, ran back to the taxi.

"If the sunflowers aren't one minute away we are heading back to the ship," Martin commanded.

The sunflower fields were a little further down the road. They were exquisite.

"Would you like to see the town? It is 10 minutes down the road."

Martin answered for me.

"We have to get back to the ship. It's leaving at 6:00 and it's 4:00 now."

There is a reason I have not mentioned the price of the taxi. We had negotiated a fee for taking us to Aix and bringing us back to the ship. I had foolishly not negotiated the price for our lavender/sunflower excursion. Why would we? It was only 10 minutes farther.

We arrived back at the dock in Marseille at 5:30. Mani announced that the trip had cost 800 euros. We only had 200 euros.

"No problem," said Mani. "You and your daughter can wait here while your husband goes to the ship to get more money."

"What a good idea!" I replied, realizing that Molly and I were being held hostage.

Martin glared at me and hurried back to the ship while Molly and I waited in the taxi.

"Did you like the lavender?" asked Mani.

"Oh yes." I said, thinking, "Not 800 euros worth."

Martin ran back to the taxi with the money and Mani released us. We just made it back to the ship on time and Martin and Molly eventually forgave me. At least I have the photos that prove we were there. Or at least I had them. I have been unable to locate them on my phone. When I bought a new phone, I'm not sure they transferred. Some things were just never meant to be. This might have been one of them.

In writing this book, I've noticed that, describing this period of my life, my memories concerning my family are much more vivid than my memories concerning my work. I do love being a comedian, but it changed from something I thought about every day into something I thought about twice a week. Maybe it has to do with my age, maybe it has to do with my illness, but the arbitrary nature of show business is a pale second to the arbitrary nature of life. I don't think it requires a psychologist to explain what had happened to me. In my youth, I had used the camaraderie of backstage Broadway and comedy clubs to create the family atmosphere that was missing from my family home. Once I had a real family with Martin and Molly, my on-stage life took second-place to my off-stage life. I hope you agree that's emotionally healthy. Similarly, I suspect my interest in real estate stems from a desire to build a home diametrically opposite to the troubled house I grew up in. In that quest, I'm lucky I found a like-minded companion in Martin.

In Las Vegas, I was still sharing a theater at the Venetian with Joan Rivers, Tim Allen and David Spade, but the Laguna Playhouse now became my New Year's Eve gig. It was perfect for me because the theatre celebrates New Year's at 9:00 (midnight in New York) and I observed the countdown and the dropping of the ball in Times Square in coordination with the huge television screen on stage. It was a perfect December 31st booking because I could be in bed by 10:00 and watch other people have fun on television. Watching other people have fun is more fun for me than actually having the fun.

Our relationship with the Laguna Playhouse gave Martin a new idea. Why not write a play? My first novel, *Tickled Pink*, had been well-received when it was published in 2001. Martin decided to turn it into a play for the Playhouse. *Tickled Pink* is about a young girl who moves to New York to become a comedian. Sound familiar? It is a semi-autobiographic novel about stand-up comedy in the 80s. It was a little strange casting a person to play young me, but we found a fabulous young actress in Los Angeles named Emma Fassler. We also found an equally-fabulous young actress named Annie Abrams to play a fictionalized version of my friend Charlene.

I was also in the play. I played three different parts, which was quite a challenge. I played an over the hill actress, a clueless waitress and, the most difficult part, a controlling mother. The controlling part came rather easily. The hard part was the German accent. I am notoriously terrible at accents, but after coaching from a fellow cast member, Robert Yacko, I got the hang of it.

The play was a success and we had offers to stage it elsewhere, but Martin and I learned an important lesson. A play with a cast of ten people is expensive to produce. After you fly the people, house the people, pay the people, it is difficult to make the balance sheet work. Our next play had a cast of two.

It's not easy being a teenager today. I feel a little sorry for my daughter. She recently sprained both of her optic nerves by rolling her eyes at me.

She used to listen to me. What happened to that? Now she only takes the advice of her peers, so I give her friend Isabella ten dollars a week to tell her to stand up straight.

Twenty-four

As I entered my sixth decade, I still loved writing jokes and performing my act, but I also enjoyed, cooking, walking Twinkle and being a wife and mother. There are many different types of people who enter show business and certainly for varied reasons, but I have narrowed the types down to two because this is my book and nobody can tell me not to. Here are the types: those who live to be in show business and those who view show business as a living.

Today I am the latter type. I love what I do and that people still like to see me do it, but I also love when I go to see the football games at Molly's school or binge-watch British murder mysteries with Martin. One of my favorite things is jingling my dog's leash in the morning and watching her bop down the stairs. I always admired Joan Rivers for her talent and tenacity, but her determination to work constantly, even though she was certainly financially secure, always baffled me. Since Joan and I alternated in a theater at the Venetian, we shared a stage manager. Al Colosi is another tough guy who loves his dogs. Before every show he shared with me stories and pictures of his two hairy babies, Carmine and Marie. He told me a story that exemplifies the love Joan Rivers had for being on camera. Al went up to Joan's suite to walk her down to the theater. He knocked on her door, she opened it and said, "Knock on my door and I'll open it again."

"Why?" asked Al.

"So I can film it," Joan replied.

Of all the qualities a person can possess, I think one of the most valuable is being able to appreciate what you have. There was an extremely successful entertainer in Las Vegas I knew and admired. He was selling out his theater every night and had a lovely family, but he could never accept the fact that he wasn't famous outside of Las Vegas and eventually it destroyed him.

One of my first friends at Catch a Rising Star was an immensely-talented comedian named Richard Jeni. Remember, I was working for Martin, with Richard and Larry Amoros, another amazing comedy mind, on the Gold Coast of Australia when Martin and I first got together? I was still in my exercise phase and was swimming 100 laps a day in the hotel pool. Richard accused me of being the slowest swimmer he had ever seen and claimed he burned more calories than I did reading a magazine while drinking a margarita. We worked on comedy material together and bonded over our love of writing jokes. Richard eventually got his own situation comedy on television. He had worked hard for this opportunity, but unfortunately the show wasn't a success. However, live he was still awesome. But he could never come to terms with the undoubtedly successful comedy career he had. He would frequently call Martin, and I'm sure other show business people, for hours of advice about how to move his career forward. Everybody who knew Richard was shocked when we heard the news that he had committed suicide. No doubt there were other mental factors involved with his deadly decision, but I don't think show business helped.

This probably isn't going to be a popular thought, but I'm going to say it anyway. I'm not sure about the phrase, "Never give up on your dream." What if your dream is making you miserable? What if you are in an abusive relationship with your dream? Why can't you alter your dream? Or at least, modify it?

I've known many people who couldn't give up the dream of being A Broadway Star. At some point, you have to look around and realize, it's not going to happen. My happiest friends are the ones who changed or adapted their dream. I'd always wanted to have my own situation comedy because I thought I could be good at it and it would be fun. I realized, after three busted pilots, that I was going to have to change my dream. All of the decisions being made regarding my life on television were out of my control.

People still ask me, "Why didn't you ever do a TV series?"

Here's the answer: I tried. Ultimately, it wasn't my decision.

Sometimes you have to change direction. Success on your own terms is certainly the most satisfying. Plus, the irony is not lost on me that the price of working seven days a week on a situation comedy about a fictitious family would probably have been at the cost of my real family.

I wrote this joke in my late twenties: "I don't understand why people panic when they get lost. I never panic when I get lost. I just change where it is I want to go."

It was more pertinent than I realized.

I was offered another comedy special by Showtime. I didn't feel that I had enough new material to fill an hour and I didn't want to go back on the road to develop material. Staying with Molly, Martin and Twinkle was my priority. Martin and I came up with a plan to have me host a special called *Rita Rudner and 3 Potential Ex-Husbands*. It featured me hosting and three funny, inappropriate male comedians. The idea was that I would do 15 minutes up front and then introduce the men: David Gee, Allan Stephan and John Fox.

I'm not sure that this mixture of me, David, Allan, and John worked as well as we would have liked. We wanted to blend all different types of comedy together. We may have made a milkshake with conflicting ingredients. I think audiences who come to see me find harsher styles of comedy a bit jarring and audiences who like harsher styles of comedy find me a bit bland. We had a great time filming the special. My favorite bit was at the end when we all sat around and traded comedian stories. Unfortunately, one of the comedians, John Fox died only a few weeks after the special was made. I'm glad I got the chance to know him.

A strange offer came from a producer in England, asking me to star in a two person play in London's West End. Martin and I both read the play and liked it, but it was in London. The minimum commitment was initially three months and then three more months if it was a hit. We didn't want to take Molly out of school and leave Twinkle for that length of time.

"What if you go over first, and then I'll join you for a week, here and there?" Martin suggested. "I could get a new wife here and then maybe when you come back we could all live together. Problem solved."

Martin is certainly a problem solver extraordinaire. We came up with another idea. After four years, we had finally completed our beach house and the Laguna Playhouse was only ten minutes away. What if the producer agreed to try the play out there? We could live in one of our homes, Molly could continue school and Martin would not have to find a second wife. In fact, he could direct the play.

Karl Sydow, the producer, agreed to our proposal, as did the Laguna Playhouse. The play needed some rewriting. Many of the references had to be changed to make sense in the USA, so the playwright, David Ambrose, was flown to America. The three of us worked on the play for two weeks and then we went into rehearsal.

I had never done a two person play before. It's scary. When the other person in the play stops talking, you always have to have something to say. Luckily, my co-star, Charles Shaughnessy, was much more talented and reliable than I was. Charles and Martin had been friends at university, and Charles had, of course, enjoyed a big TV success on *The Nanny* with Fran Drescher.

The play was called *Act 3*... The premise was this: a woman whose husband is becoming distant adopts an online persona to communicate with him and finds out things about her husband that she would rather not know. The shocking fact was that this was a true story and David wrote the original script in conjunction with the actual woman who lived through the experience in France.

I started studying the script two months before rehearsal began. My part was tricky because half of what I was memorizing were letters written to my husband in an alternate persona. Molly tried to help me memorize the play but often, I was so off-base, we would just dissolve into laughter.

The opening night was terrifying for me and if the audience had been given a little more information, it would have been terrifying for them as well. Karl, the UK producer, couldn't believe it when he spotted me still studying the script in the car as Martin and I drove up to the theater. Martin wasn't allowed to talk to me at all in the car. I just concentrated on what I had to say and in which persona I had to say it.

We had three previews and, luckily, I made my worst mistake before opening night. It was a matinee when I temporarily lost concentration and recited the last letter of the play at the beginning of the opening of the second act. Poor Charles tried to steer me back but nothing was making any sense. I had cut 50 pages. I had to do something both unwise and unconventional. I stopped the show and said to the audience, "I'm so sorry. I have to confess I've recited the wrong letter and we are going to have to begin this scene again." I looked over in the wings and saw an unamused husband/director.

"My husband is standing in the wings and he is not happy. Martin, would you like to come out and say a few words?"

Martin came on stage and just said, "I don't believe it!" And then he exited.

Someone from the audience shouted, "Why don't you just read the letters instead of memorizing them?"

Indeed, I could have read the letters because part of the play took place at a desk with me looking at a computer but that would be like reading my act instead of memorizing it.

"Because," I replied, "you came here to see a show. Not someone reading. Even though I messed up, isn't this more fun?"

"Yes," the audience replied.

I begged the audience not to tell anyone what had just happened, I apologized to my co-star Charles and we began the scene again. After the show, the playwright, David Ambrose, came over to me.

"Again, I'm sorry," I said, mortified.

"I loved it. It was one of my favorite moments in the theater!"

I don't think he really meant that remark, but it was sweet of him and I was eternally grateful that my lapse occurred before opening night. I never made that egregious a mistake again, but often Charles said that when he looked in my eyes, he could see me searching for what came next.

"Rita, I saw a whole bunch of empty there tonight in that third scene, but somehow you pulled it out. Scary!!!"

The play was very well received, but Martin and I didn't think the premise was unique enough to risk the wrath of the critics in New York. Doing the play did give me more confidence in my ability to act. Confidence is something I've always struggled with. Before every performance I had to remember my mantra; if other people can do it, I can do it too. Although there were a few moments when I almost didn't do it.

At the play's conclusion, we returned to Las Vegas. I was pushing a cart around a supermarket when my phone rang. It was Senator Harry Reid.

"Hi, Rita. Harry. Have you ever considered running for public office?"

"Excuse me?"

"There's a Nevada representative seat up for election. I think you should run."

"I think you've phoned the wrong number, Senator Reid. This is Rita Rudner."

"I know. We've tested you. You have virtually zero negatives. People really like you. You'd have a terrific chance of winning."

"I can't go to Washington. I have a daughter."

"How old is she?"

"Fifteen."

"She doesn't need you anymore. You can do it."

"But I don't want to."

"Just talk to your campaign manager."

"I HAVE A CAMPAIGN MANAGER?!" I shrieked.

"Purely provisional."

It was a tempting offer, but I decided to decline. What if I had run and won? I would have experienced the Trump presidency close up. I would be brushing shoulders now with Marjorie Taylor Greene, Jim Jordan and Matt Gaetz. I think I made the right call.

Limiting my schedule in Las Vegas was working for us. I started playing once in a while at the Red Rock Casino in Summerlin and we still spent a lot of time in our lovely home-base overlooking the Strip. However, I also committed to three more cruises – one on the French Riviera, one in the Pacific and one in Alaska with Oprah Winfrey. I did a three-week tour in Florida. We visited Israel. I performed concerts across the country, some with Brad Garrett, some with Louie Anderson, some with Paul Reiser, some with Robert Klein and some alone.

One show I did was with Molly and Michael McDonald, who is one of my all-time favorite singers. The adoption agency in Los Angeles that had helped us adopt Molly was holding a benefit. The organizers asked me to emcee and also asked 15-year-old Molly, whom they followed on YouTube, to sing one of her songs. Called "Who Are You?" it seemed strikingly appropriate to her adoption story. Molly loved meeting and performing with Michael and relished the opportunity of giving back to the agency that had helped her before she was even born, but her favorite thing about the entire evening was that she had the services of her own guitar roadie. He tuned her guitar for her and made sure it was in place for her performance. She'd never felt so special.

In 2017, I was told I was to be presented with a Casino Entertainment Legend Award at the Hard Rock Hotel in Las Vegas. Sounded like a nice night out, until, a week before the ceremony was to take place, a madman shot up the Route 91 Harvest music festival. Las Vegas was numb with shock. The next day, we drove past Mandalay Bay and saw the gaping window wound and flapping curtains from where the shots had been fired.

The organizers of the Casino Entertainment Legend Awards were desperate not to cancel, so I reluctantly agreed to show up as planned. It was a very muted evening. Quite a few of the people present had been at the music festival and helped pull wounded people to safety. They were still visibly traumatized. I know Las Vegas is a silly place, but the great joy of it for locals is that it is a city with a small town feel at heart. Everyone knows everyone and when tragedy strikes, its residents can be relied upon to offer total support to both each other and visitors. Simply put, some of the nicest people in my life are the ones I've worked with in Las Vegas.

I've also, it has to be said, met some kooks there. There was Molly's highly-respected and lauded pediatrician, who apparently stole placentas to use in an illegitimate stem cell implant business. There was the neighbor who ran a Ponzi scheme that ended when the FBI arrested him while he was hiding underneath a car in our underground car park. And there was the woman who regularly got so drunk at our swimming pool that she would tip Molly, thinking she was a 7-year-old waitress. I saw this woman limping towards me one night when I returned from a performance.

"Are you okay?" I asked.

"I was crossing the street and I fell off my Jimmy Choos," she wailed.

It happens.

Comedy Central asked me to take part in a show called *This Is Not Happening* that was being recorded in a strip club in Los Angeles. Why not? The producers didn't want me to do stand-up.

They wanted me to tell a true story from my life. This was a challenging assignment for me, because telling a story is not necessarily in my comedy wheelhouse. My comedic metronome, no doubt influenced by my years of ballet, is all about rhythm and brevity. Eventually, I decided to tell a story that had just happened, when Twinkle had apparently found a missing cat while I was walking her. It's on the internet, if you want to see how I told it. Last time I searched for it, it had been viewed over 700,000 times. No, I don't understand how that happens either

I was invited to write and perform another one-hour comedy special by a Los Angeles production company. I took a few gigs in clubs on the road to try out new material. The special was called *A Tale of Two Dresses* because I couldn't decide what to wear. My goal in this special was to make my material more truthful and organic. I've always admired comedians who pull an audience in with a story. I came to comedy learning how to write jokes, but the experience of being in plays has helped me become more emotionally involved with my material and telling the anecdote on *This Is Not Happening* helped too. I feel my comedy is never done. There is always a way I can improve it and I will never stop trying. Our daughter also made an appearance at the end of that special. She played the guitar and sang a song she wrote to a photo montage of me, Martin and her growing old together. In my opinion, Molly has aged the most. Again, there are clips of this special on the internet. One of them has been viewed 1.3 million times. No, I don't understand how that happens either.

I love being married. It's so great to find that one special person you want to annoy for the rest of your life.

Twenty-five

Remember when Martin said he should stop coming up with ideas as we demolished the Toaster? Well, he'd evidently forgotten that, because he and a very talented local musician and friend, Jason Feddy, decided to take a crack at a musical. Jason wrote the songs while Martin and I wrote the script. We based it on a play we had written in Las Vegas years before to raise funds for a local community theater called The Little Theatre. The premise was simple: two strangers have double-booked a room in Las Vegas on a sold-out weekend and are forced to share it despite their immediate antipathy towards each other. We called it *Two's A Crowd*. Martin and I are both enormous fans of the plays of Neil Simon, and had spent time with Neil and his then wife Diane in Los Angeles before we were married. Neil told me this story about their wedding: his future wife had been busily preparing herself for her special day and he had not seen her since the early morning. She'd had her hair done, her makeup applied and was wearing a spectacular gown. As she walked down the aisle towards him, he whispered to his best man, "Wrong woman." Martin and I had always admired Neil's writing and we wanted to attempt the specificity of one of his premises as well as the wit of his fast-moving dialogue.

We first tried out *Two's A Crowd* at the Laguna Playhouse for two weeks. Jason assembled a band and Martin assembled a cast. Our two old improvising friends from *BOO!* and *Thanks,* Kelly Holden Bashar and Brian Lohmann, agreed to join us, as did the wonderful Davis Gaines, best known for over 2,000 performances as the Phantom in Andrew Lloyd Webber's *Phantom of The Opera*. During the run at the Playhouse, we were approached about bringing the production to New York the following summer. Davis's prior

256

commitments meant he couldn't join us in Manhattan, so he was replaced by Robert Yacko, who had appeared in *Tickled Pink*.

Two's A Crowd played at 59E59 Theaters in the heart of Manhattan for seven weeks in the summer of 2019. After almost 40 years, I had come full circle and was back singing and almost dancing in New York. Martin, Molly and I moved into a residential hotel and rented two inter-connecting one- bedroom apartments. It was Molly's idea of heaven. She had her own apartment, but we were there if she needed us. Very often, we would take out Chinese food, go over to her apartment for dinner and make her clean up the dishes. Please don't alert the authorities. Molly helped out backstage as an intern at night (she was on summer vacation) and during the day explored Manhattan in the same way as I had 50 years earlier. A variety of her friends flitted through town and stayed with us, whilst many of my friends came to see the show and then have dinner with us afterwards. We met my ballet friends Lisa and Bonnie, together with their mother Rose, one day for lunch, and Lisa pulled me to one side as we were leaving the restaurant. She wasn't feeling well and was nervous that her cancer had returned. After seeing our show, she was off to Singapore, where we'd had dinner together years before, to recreate a Balanchine ballet. She was only there a week before she was forced to fly back to San Francisco for further tests.

My childhood ballet friend, Charlene, had a similar tale to tell. Her ovarian cancer had metastasized and her treatment at Sloan-Kettering was creating unpleasant side effects. The fact that this disease is usually discovered too late to reverse its course is such a tragedy. One of the major upsides to being in New York that summer was that the two of us got to spend more time together than we had since we were kids. We both suspected that the clock was ticking, but we left our fears unspoken and enjoyed as many lunches, walks and shared memories as we could.

The show was by and large well-received. The critics are so different from the days when I was dancing on Broadway. Then, I'd seen a bad review in the New York Times assassinate a show as good as *Mack and Mabel*. Now there are so many critical outlets, especially online, and the Times doesn't wield the sort of power and readership it did in the 20th century. I have learned not to take reviews too seriously. It doesn't matter what critics say and whether or not you win an award if you have done your best. That being said, it is always a better feeling to not be dragged through the verbal mud and I was pleased when the Times said I had, "*Spiky-soft charisma paired with immaculate timing*" and Time Out said I put "*the sex back into sexagenarian,*" which I think is a cousin to a compliment. Martin and I both knew the play was unfashionable – full of snappy jokes and aimed clearly at an older audience – and we hadn't expected it to have much of a life past the summer. However, we were pleasantly surprised when a well-known Broadway producer showed interest in transferring it to a larger theatre some time in 2020, when Molly would be at college. Turns out "an older audience" is exactly who supports theater today, especially women, who are often the one in a partnership who make the plans and buy the tickets.

Before we could discuss a transfer, I had some concert bookings around the country I had to honor and I had also agreed to appear in an upcoming production of Neil Simon's *Barefoot in the Park* back at the Laguna Playhouse, replacing Melanie Griffith who was forced to drop out. We were halfway through that run, when Covid 19 closed California down. Suddenly I was barefoot in the parking lot. New York had already closed down, meaning an off-Broadway transfer of *Two's A Crowd* wasn't happening either. Like everyone else in show business, we retreated to our house, bought masks and hand sanitizer and rooted for the medical professionals.

It's now 2022. I'm about to do my first run of stand-up performances in almost two years, as well as perform at the wonderful philanthropist Lois Pope's *Lady in Red* Gala in Palm Beach. Molly started performing live before me: last year she opened for Jewel as well as for Train, Rick Springfield and Sammy Hagar. She's now studying for a Bachelor of Music degree at college and having a ball. Looking at her now, at 19, I realize how crazy my father's decision was to let me leave home at 15. Once, when he was living in Las Vegas, one of our friends asked him, "If Rita left the house so young, who raised her?"

My dad replied, "Rita Carol raised herself."

I guess in a way that's true, but in another way, I owe my sense of balance to my friends, my psycho-analyst, my husband, my daughter and the people I met along the way. Both good and bad. I also think I owe my sense of responsibility to my dogs. Even when no one else needed or loved me, my dogs always did.

Going through a cancer diagnosis was certainly a challenge but, in the spirit of turning a setback into something positive, it has been a source of satisfaction to help some of my friends who have had similar problems. I've been able to let them know what to expect and when and how to deal with mysterious side effects.

Lisa, Charlene and I had all noticed that chemotherapy negatively affected our fingerprints. The three of us agreed to one day get together and commit a crime; the police would never be able to track us down. Sadly, before our trio could break the law, Lisa and Charlene lost their battles. Magnificent ballerinas both, Lisa with the New York City Ballet and Charlene with the Joffrey, I say hello to their photos every day.

Over the past 12 months, many people mentioned in this book have also departed: Stephen Sondheim, Hal Prince, Jerry Herman, Sheldon Adelson, Harry Reid, Betty White, Bobby Morse. My friend Harriet, whose mother Selma used to make clothes with my mother for us both to wear, passed away tragically. My comedy friends Bob Saget, Louie Anderson and Gilbert Gottfried also left the stage way too soon.

Last year, we sold our apartment in Las Vegas and moved full-time to our house in California. 13-year-old Twinkle left us on New Year's Eve, which was tough. Molly's on the other side of the country. We seem to be in a pattern of change that the pandemic exacerbated, as it has for so many.

I was so distraught over Twinkle I wasn't sure whether I had another dog in me, but my friend Ava told me about a rescue organization called The Little Red Dog. A sweet dog with a broken leg had just been rescued from the streets of Los Angeles and was being fostered by Ava's friend, Robin. I went to visit the dog, fell in love with her and a few months ago adorable Betsy moved in with us. Turns out, I do have another dog in me. I'm looking forward to "The Betsy Years."

So, there we have it. Consider yourself up to date on the Rita Rudner story. Nobody knows how much time any of us has left, but if you are what you leave in the world, I would hope to leave kindness and laughter and a daughter who loves me. That's what was left by my mother, and I dedicate this book to her.

My husband doesn't travel with me, but I never worry about him cheating on me when I'm away because he has his whole business on his computer. So, before I leave, I always erase an important file.

Up-to-date information on Rita Rudner can be found at her website www.ritarudner.com

Information on The Little Red Dog non-profit organization can be found at https://thelittlereddog.org

Information on Marty Hennessey's Inspiring Children Foundation can be found at https://inspiringchildren.org